# GOD ON THE STREETS OF GOTHAM

# GOD
## ON THE STREETS OF
# GOTHAM

WHAT THE BIG SCREEN **BATMAN**
CAN TEACH US ABOUT **GOD** AND OURSELVES

# PAUL ASAY

TYNDALE HOUSE PUBLISHERS, INC.
CAROL STREAM, ILLINOIS

Visit Tyndale online at www.tyndale.com.

*TYNDALE* and Tyndale's quill logo are registered trademarks of Tyndale House Publishers, Inc.

*God on the Streets of Gotham: What the Big Screen Batman Can Teach Us about God and Ourselves*

Designed by Daniel Farrell

Edited by Jonathan Schindler

The author is represented by Alive Communications, Inc., 7680 Goddard St., Suite 200, Colorado Springs, CO 80920. www.alivecommunications.com.

**Library of Congress Cataloging-in-Publication Data**

Asay, Paul.
    God on the streets of Gotham : what the big screen Batman can teach us about God and ourselves / by Paul Asay.
        p. cm.
    ISBN 978-1-4143-6640-1 (sc)
 1. Batman films—History and criticism. 2. Motion pictures—Religious aspects. I. Title.
    PN1995.9.B34A83 2012
    791.43′682—dc23   2012000820

Printed in the United States of America

| 18 | 17 | 16 | 15 | 14 | 13 | 12 |
|----|----|----|----|----|----|----|
| 7  | 6  | 5  | 4  | 3  | 2  | 1  |

*To Mom and Dad, who never gave up on me.*

*You're my heroes.*

# CONTENTS

# INTRODUCTION

**IF YOU READ** this book and want someone to blame for it, waggle your finger at William Hanna and Joseph Barbera. It's all their fault.

When I was a kid, I practically lived for Saturday morning cartoons. I'd leap out of bed, run to the TV room (my footie PJs slipping on the linoleum), flip on the television, and watch cartoons until my mom made me stop—and almost all of them were from Hanna-Barbera's über-prolific (and ultra-cheap) animation studios. I loved 'em all, from *Hong Kong Phooey* to *Speed Buggy* to *Captain Caveman and the Teen Angels*.

But nothing could compare to the excellent awesomeness of *Super Friends*.

To my five-year-old self, *Super Friends* was the pinnacle of cartoon quality—*Citizen Kane* with Froot Loops commercials. I was mesmerized by these caped heroes and heroines: Superman with his super strength, super speed, and that super curly lock of hair on his forehead; Wonder Woman with her nifty Lasso of Truth and awesome Invisible Plane; Aquaman with his . . . um . . . well, okay, Aquaman's ability to talk with fish and ride huge seahorses seemed a little impractical to me, even at age five. Really, how many diabolical crime sprees take place in large bodies of water?

And then, of course, there were Batman and Robin. Sure, they might not have had the outlandish super abilities their Justice League brethren did, but what they lacked in super strength, stealth planes, or the ability to talk with sea anemones, they made up for with technological savvy, clever wordplay, and sheer gumption. They made a great team. If you're going to be trapped in an old gold mine or stranded on a faraway planet or thrown back in time by a gigantic space ray, it's nice to have company.

It's easy to see the appeal of these guys. For kids like me who could barely scoot a chair under a table, superheroes were the epitome of everything we wanted to be but weren't: strong, brave, good, and strong. Powerful, too. Did I mention strong? No one would dare tell Superman when it was time to go to bed or force Batman to eat his veggies. And naturally, being the sort of boy who hated both bedtime and beets, it wasn't long before I started slipping into superhero fanaticism. The first coloring book I remember having was themed around Batman's brave exploits. I'd draw my own *Super Friends* stories. Every time I got together with my best friend, Terry, we'd shove rolled-up sock balls into our sleeves, tie towels around our necks, and zip around the backyard pretending to be Superman and Batman, righting imaginary wrongs and saving innocent stuffed animals wherever we might find them.

But every superhero experiences his share of adversity—especially those who are less than four feet tall and still a decade away from earning a driver's license. There comes a time when they must face an adversary too big and too powerful for them to tackle. They must deal with a threat that causes even the strongest of superheroes to quake in their primary-colored boots.

I called mine, simply, "Daddy."

## THE BOY WONDER AND THE DAD OF DOOM

My father didn't send me to bed without my utility belt or take away my Bat Big Wheel. He went way beyond that. He told me that superheroes were bad. And then he said I couldn't have anything to do with them anymore. It was like he pointed an anti-happiness ray gun at me and pulled the trigger.

Had I been up on real superhero lore back then (rather than just a steady diet of *Super Friends*), I might have interpreted my dad's resistance to my heroic calling as a betrayal akin to Grecian tragedy. After all, my father was my hero—so strong he could carry me on his shoulders, so fast I could never get away from him when bath time came. He could talk like Mickey Mouse, tell jokes better than Tim Conway, and when the car battery died, he could push the car all by himself—with Mom and me in it. He was a *fireman*, for cryin' out loud! Forget Batman: when I really thought about what I wanted to be when I grew up, I wanted to be my dad.

And there was a time when he seemed to share my

keenness for superheroes. He incorporated them into my bedtime stories (at my request), helped me build a Superman model (okay, he built it for me), and one time even designed a big, flannel *S* that I could pin to my shirt.

But something happened to my dad—something took him over, body and soul—and my world was never quite the same.

That "something" was Jesus.

See, Jesus didn't just gently ask my dad to "come, follow me." It was like Jesus took him by the collar and hollered, "YOU'RE GONNA FOLLOW ME, BUDDY!" And my dad followed like paparazzi follow Lindsay Lohan. And he took the whole family with him.

It was tough, or so I hear. My mom was already a Christian, but her Presbyterian brand of faith was pretty traditional, full of a steady dose of hymns and potluck suppers. So when my dad started speaking in tongues and pouring wine down the sink, she didn't have a great frame of reference for what was going on. And when my dad's enthusiasm got us kicked out of our hometown church and ostracized by most of her friends, well, Mom was one loud "Hallelujah!" away from heading back home to her mother's, taking me and my little sister with her.

I was still pretty young—about six or seven—so I was blessedly unaware of how close I was to growing up fatherless. All I knew was that we switched churches and I didn't see Terry (who was Presbyterian) nearly as much. But the biggest, most cataclysmic change was that I wasn't allowed to watch *Super Friends* anymore. My tiny collection of superhero comics and

Colorforms sets disappeared. My solitary Batman record vanished. It was as if a big hunk of kryptonite had been dropped in my bedroom, dispelling all superheroes and sidekicks with nary a "fwooping" sound.

The whole superhero cleansing episode left me more bewildered than sad. My dad explained to me how I should have just one hero—Jesus—and while I didn't really understand how anyone could ever confuse Jesus with Batman, I mostly moved on. I was thirty-five pounds of scrawniness with not even a batarang to my name. What else could I do?

Fast-forward thirtysomething years, and now I've written a book about Batman and Jesus. In it, I often mention them together, in the very same sentence (like this one)—which either completely refutes my father's fears or absolutely confirms them.

My dad and I chuckle about those crazy days now, but the truth is he probably feels a smidge more guilt over the whole superhero cleansing thing than he should. Even with my love of superheroes still obviously intact, I can see where he was coming from. Here was a man trying to figure out what being "on fire for the Lord" should look like in real, everyday life. That's not an easy thing for any of us to navigate, and it certainly wasn't for my father, given that the Bible does not tell us explicitly how to view animated superheroes. Are they idols? Reflections of greater spiritual truths? Do they show kids that it's good to stand up for what's right and what you believe in, or do they teach that violence is the answer to almost any problem? These are pretty legitimate questions, I think—ones we'd do well to ask today, quite frankly. We shouldn't accept anything this world offers without some thought. And, of course, my dad's decision was complicated (as all these things tend to be) by not just who he was at the time, but how *he* was raised too.

## BATMAN BAGGAGE

When my dad was a kid, lots of folks were buzzing about how horrible comic books were for the juvenile mind—how violent and sexualized and inherently corrupting they were. The most obvious counterstrike against comics came with 1954's *Seduction of the Innocent* by psychologist Fredric Wertham, who made the case that Superman was a fascist, Wonder Woman was into bondage, and Batman and Robin were gay lovers. But comics were of grave concern to parents and psychologists well before that, as a 1948 issue of the *American Journal of Psychotherapy* makes clear. Several psychologists participated in a symposium titled "The Psychopathology of Comic Books," in which the new medium fared very poorly indeed.

"If there is only one violent picture per page—and there are usually more—every city child who was six years old in 1938 has by now absorbed an absolute minimum of eighteen thousand pictorial beatings, shootings, stranglings, blood-puddles and torturings-to-death, from comic books alone," wrote Gerson Legman for the symposium. Lumping in the harmful influence of radio and movies, Legman said that "the effect—and there are those who think it has been a conscious intention—has been to raise up an entire generation of adolescents who have felt, thousands upon thousands of times, all the sensations and emotions of committing murder, except pulling the trigger."

And in some ways, these cautious psychotherapists and parents were right: comic books were (and are) violent. They did (and do) feature some pretty sexually charged images. Critics would say they excuse vigilantism and posit that as long as you can beat up your adversary, everything is A-OK. And let's be honest, *I* might even say that. I work for an organization that examines all sorts of secular media, from movies to video games, from a Christian point of view, and I'm constantly writing about how problematic depictions of sex and violence can be on young minds (and on old ones too). The images we see affect us in ways both overt and subtle, and we might not ever notice that these things are influencing us at all.

Modern superhero movies are all the more problematic. In my gig, I'm always called to be mindful of Philippians 4:8, which tells us all to concentrate on "what is true, and honorable, and right, and pure, and lovely, and admirable." And while you could make an argument that Batman can often be noble and right and admirable, he also can be brutal and angry and not very admirable at all. And when you throw in the death-by-pencil stuff in *The Dark Knight*, the modern incarnation of the Batman universe simply doesn't feel very Philippians-like.

And let's not forget my dad's primary concern, the whole issue of superheroes being a replacement for Christ. Maybe to some six-year-olds, Superman seems like a divine force— as cool as any angel and maybe even cooler than Jesus. After all, Superman can lift train engines, stop bullets, and fly.

Jesus performed some neat miracles and all, but feeding five thousand people isn't quite as dramatic as *melting steel with your eyes*! And then, even though Jesus is the Son of God, he allowed himself to die. As adults we see the significance of Christ's sacrifice, but kids, without a firm grasp on the concepts of sin and grace but really familiar with the second-grade bully, long for a savior who can conk a few skulls. Even the disciples thought that's what Jesus was going to do—right up to his crucifixion.

So if you're reading this right now and questioning what business I have taking a dark, secular superhero and turning him into a Christian role model, let me stress that I get your concerns. I've thought through them and wrestled with them and prayed about them more than was strictly helpful.

And I've set them, gently and respectfully, aside.

Here's why.

## SOMETHING SUPER

I believe we can find evidence of God everywhere. We are his creation, after all, and who we are and what we do cannot help but carry his mark. From the loftiest mountain to the lowliest weed, everything around us bears his autograph. And as we are God's most marvelous achievement, made in his own image, we're inherently beautiful. We can't help it. And so when we, in turn, create something—a mimicry of God's own awesome act of creation—a bit of God's life and love filters into what we mold and make, regardless of our intent.

Now, there's a flip side to this. Just as we all trace our

lineage to the mind of the Almighty, our creations are marred by the fallen world in which we live. Just as the spark of the divine is in everything, so is the taint of sin. As such, our most beautiful, our most holy of constructs are not free of the world's sour corruption, the mark of the fall. Nothing escapes it. Nothing in this world is above it.

Which makes Gotham City, the world of Batman, so illustrative in many ways of our own failed and fallen realm. Gotham's a dark place, full of shadow, corruption, and bad intentions. It's not pure or pretty, and none of the people in it are free of sin's taint. And yet underneath the grime and graffiti and dark forebode, there's goodness, too. There are those who believe there's a spark worth preserving in this desperate city. There are those who see the beauty underneath. They see the spirit of the city and believe it's still possible, somehow, to redeem it.

Sure, Batman's stomping grounds aren't always "right" or "noble" or "admirable." But neither was the world in which the apostle Paul lived back when he wrote to the Philippians. And neither is ours. We were collectively kicked out of paradise a long time ago, and perfect purity is as elusive as a unicorn carrying licorice whips. Every day, we're exposed to the imperfect, the ugly, the reality of our fallen world and our frail natures.

But is there good to be found here? Yes. Even the stained world of Gotham still contains moments of nobility, purity, and loveliness. We can admire the admirable here; we can celebrate what's right. We can concentrate on those aspects within the city's gritty confines and perhaps uncover a spark of the divine in superherodom's gloomiest character. We won't find a *substitute* for Jesus, but we may find a *servant*—even if he doesn't fully understand it and might not always act like it.

I hope to show that Batman followed something of a sacred call, even if he didn't know exactly where that call came from. He found a special purpose, even if he didn't know who placed that purpose in front of him. He'll teach us a bit about goodness and God and our own conflicting natures, becoming an unwitting spiritual instructor. I believe we're all a little like Batman, trying to find our way in a messed-up reality and yet knowing, deep in our being, that Someone thinks we're special and that we can *be* special. Even as we plow through our very normal, non-superhero lives, we're all called for a purpose we can hardly imagine.

Perhaps when all is said and done, Batman isn't all that different from who my father was when I was six. Perhaps they're simply men who, in spite of the odds and obstacles facing them—in spite of tempting the wrath of Gotham's villains or the ire of a little boy—heard a different call and followed it the best they could.

# Chapter 1

# MASKED

*One may understand the cosmos, but never the ego; the self is more distant than any star.*
—G. K. Chesterton, *Orthodoxy*

**IT TAKES A SPECIAL PERSON** to dress up like a flying rodent. And when I say *special*, I mostly mean *weird*.

And when I say *weird*, I mean *weird for grown-ups*. My son used to wear a homemade bat outfit around the house when he was four, flapping its sewn-on wings in a desperate effort to fly around the living room. But were he still doing so today, at age twenty, I'd sit him down and encourage a less eclectic sense of fashion. It's one thing to wear a bat costume to bed; it's another to wear one to job interviews.

Granted, Bruce Wayne—Batman's moneyed alter ego—doesn't need a job. Gotham City's prominent playboy billionaire has more money under his sofa cushions than most of us have in our checking accounts. And if he ever *wanted* a job for some inexplicable reason, he owns a whole corporation full of middle managers who'd be falling all over themselves to hire him. Rich folk have more license than the rest of us to engage in, shall we say, eccentric hobbies. If Lady Gaga can dress up in meat for the occasional award ceremony, who's going to begrudge Bruce a cowl and cape?

But Bruce's eccentricity—if we can call it that—goes far deeper. When he puts on his mask and straps on his utility belt, he's not playing dress-up. In his case, clothes really do make the man. What he wears is in some critical, half-understood way more reflective of the real Bruce Wayne than his billionaire playboy facade is or could ever be. When he wears this dark guise, Bruce shoots past eccentricity and reaches beyond weird. As Batman, he flies into a dangerous, dreamlike world that at times can resemble an acid trip gone terribly awry. And he has the almost unthinkable impression that he can somehow make this nightmare landscape *better*.

This is more than a mere oddity. It's a psychosis.

Or . . . a calling.

## WHY SO SERIOUS?

Whatever you call it, Batman's been doing it for a long time. He began his career in *Detective Comics* No. 27 in May 1939, when the country was still mired in the Great Depression and the planet was speeding toward World War II. He was a dark vigilante then, suitable for those uneasy times when gangsters and crooks sometimes seemed beyond the reach of the law. For more than seventy years, he's been fighting crime and wrestling with evildoers in comics, newspapers, television, and movies, and in the imaginations of eight-year-old boys wearing tied-on capes and forty-year-old men with too much time on their hands. And while he hasn't always been the grim character he was in the beginning, he's always had a bit of an edge. Even in the colorful, campy ABC television show that popularized the character in 1966, Adam West's Caped Crusader never laughs. For him, crime fighting is serious business . . . and that's the joke.

Now, of course, West's straight-faced superhero is long gone, replaced in popular culture by Christian Bale's brooding Batman in Christopher Nolan's trilogy (*Batman Begins*, *The Dark Knight*, and *The Dark Knight Rises*). The DC Comics character is often complex and conflicted. For seventy-plus years, we've called him a hero.

But is he? And if he is, what makes him so? We've grown so used to the guy that we sometimes forget how disturbing his persona is, how disturbing it was *designed* to be. He's no cookie-cutter crime fighter with a Dudley Do-Right dimple or a Superman smile who will tell children to mind their studies, mind their parents, and always, always floss. From the very beginning, Batman has been a dark character, more at home in Gotham's shadows than its light.

So as we dive into a book that attempts to use Batman as some sort of spiritual instructor, a shadowy guide who may help us walk better in the light, it's best to remember not just who we *want* Batman to be but who he *is*. If we saw Batman on the street and didn't know who he was, we'd run away from, not toward, the guy. If we saw something like him in medieval art, we'd think he was more demon than angel.

Before the lessons begin, we must meet our instructor; we must see if this guy has anything to teach us, anything to share. Can we trust him? What if there's something not quite right underneath that cowl of his? What if he's not a superhero at all?

## IT'S A BIRD, IT'S A PLANE, IT'S A MESSIAH METAPHOR!

We all know what superheroes are supposed to be about—how they look and talk and act. Batman may arguably be the most popular superhero around these days, but when we think of a generic superhero, there's still a pretty good chance that we envision another DC Comics creation—that big dude from Metropolis with the *S* on his chest. "Now *that's* a superhero," we might say. Superman defined the word, and we know that if Superman and Batman tangled in a mixed martial arts ring, the Man of Steel would clean Batman's belfry. The guy's a rock 'em, sock 'em demigod, graced with extraterrestrial super strength, speed, and good manners. And from the very beginning, he was presented as a savior.

Superman, as we know the story today, was born Kal-El (a Hebrew-inflected name interpreted by some to mean "the voice of God") on a faraway planet destroyed in a tragic cataclysm. His parents shipped him off to Earth just before things got really nasty—not just to save the boy's life, but to send him to a world that Kal-El, in turn, could save.

"They can be a great people, Kal-El, if they wish to be,"

his father, Jor-El, tells Superman in the 2006 film *Superman Returns*. "They only lack the light to show the way. For this reason above all, their capacity for good, I have sent them you . . . my only son." Powerful, good, and incorruptible, Superman seems both Greek god and Christian saint. And in case anyone missed the metaphor up to that point, in *Superman Returns* we see him sacrifice himself for the world . . . and yet return, as it were, from the dead.

Batman, conversely, is no smiling, superhuman alien sent to save humanity. He shares very little in common with the Man of Steel. We call Batman a superhero, but he has no special abilities to speak of, no talents born of Krypton or gamma ray showers, no gifts garnered through mysterious spider bites or medical experiments gone wrong. He's a self-made man—fully human, just as we are. He's not all-powerful. He's not, as we shall see, altogether good. He is a product of our fallen world even as he strives to rise above it. He holds the seed of God's perfect creation, and yet that seed is embedded in the dirt of tragedy, temptation, sin, and corruption.

And he knows it.

"Deep down, Clark's essentially a good person," Batman admits of his super pal in the DC Comics saga *Hush*. "And deep down, I'm not."

"You either die a hero, or you live long enough to see yourself become the villain," we're told in *The Dark Knight*. In real life, we've seen countless heroes—athletes, actors, politicians, pastors—fall and crash, and Batman is complex enough, enigmatic enough, damaged enough for us to fear that he could fall too. Batman's weakness isn't kryptonite, silver, or some otherworldly thing: it's his own, very human nature. And that's part of what makes him so compelling.

Sure, Batman sometimes acts as a savior stand-in. But for the most part, he's not a Messiah figure.

He's us.

## HOLY INCONSISTENCIES, BATMAN!

Those of us who have been to Sunday school at least twice (and didn't sneak out during the songs) know at least a little about the character of Jesus—how he is the Son of God who came to Earth as a puny mortal to teach us stuff and save us from, essentially, ourselves. Jesus was both completely God and completely human, and since he was a normal guy (in a sense), he experienced most of what we normal guys and girls do: hunger, thirst, pain, sleepiness, that sort of thing.

But some of the stuff we humans do as just part of being human is, at least to my way of thinking, incompatible with the nature of being God.

Take, for instance, the concept of inconsistency. You can't accuse Jesus of being inconsistent. Granted, he had his moments and moods. He could be angry or gentle or sad or even a little exasperated. But while we might read about him telling stories in one chapter and turning over tables in the next, he was always Jesus, if that makes sense. Nothing he did was ever out of character, outside the mold of who we know Jesus to be.

We, on the other hand, are wildly inconsistent.

Oh, sure, we try to convince ourselves that we know who

we are. We tell our friends that we're this type of guy or not that sort of girl. We tell everyone what great senses of humor we have or how much we care for the poor—traits that we feel get down to the core of what we're all about (or who we'd like to be). And if we're not so sure about who we are, we have a whole slew of personality tests designed to tell us.

For instance, the folks at Myers & Briggs tell me I'm an INFP, which means I'm a shy, artistic, touchy-feely type—the kind of person who might write a book about the spirituality of superheroes. But they'd be shocked if they knew I was nearly thrown out of one of my son's soccer games for getting, shall we say, overly enthusiastic. My math teachers, who knew me as the guy who'd doodle all over my notes, would be surprised to know that I regularly crunch a whole bunch of wonky stats while trying to compile a fantasy football team.

Truth is, I'm not always an INFP. Sometimes I might be a more gregarious ENFP or a more judgmental INFJ, and sometimes I can go totally against my character and do a good impression of an ESTJ. On really bad days, I resemble an ICBM. Sure, we might have an inkling of who we are and how we'll react. Those personality tests can be pretty revealing. But all those Myers-Briggs letters can't convey the whole story, and all the rules and inclinations and character types we set for ourselves are littered with exceptions. I think I have a great sense of humor but sometimes don't get obvious jokes. I run three hours, then grab a Sausage McMuffin at McDonald's.

And we're all like that. The most patient among us can snap at a barista. The most cautious among us sometimes take up hang gliding. We have more faces than the Rolex factory, more personas than the cast of *Saturday Night Live*. Sometimes it would seem that we're not one person but several—forever flexing from one to the next, changing colors like a Las Vegas fountain.

Batman fits right in with the rest of us. Sometimes he seems hardly the same superhero. One decade he's a dark loner, the next he's a veritable family man, surrounded by batwomen, batgirls, and batpets. In one graphic novel, he's a wreck, torn asunder by compulsion and neurosis. In another, he's a rock, a pillar of goodness and virtue. You're never quite sure what you're going to get with Batman—just like us.

## THE MEN IN THE MASKS

Batman's inconsistencies aren't just born of outside influences—the writers, artists, actors, and directors who have all had a hand in shaping the superhero's mythic arc over the years and the demands of the readers and viewers who consume his stories. He's a complex, often contradictory character *within* these various works too—at one turn the billionaire playboy, at another the dark vigilante, at still another a man unsure, seemingly puzzled by who he is and what he's become, still searching for his parents' approval.

"What am I doing, Alfred?" he asks in 1993's *Batman: Mask of the Phantasm*, one of countless times he's turned to his loyal, ever-present valet for advice. Having fallen in love, he's in anguish over whether it's okay to be a masked vigilante *and* a significant other. "This isn't part of the plan!" he says.

It's not the first time Batman has surprised even himself. No wonder we're not always sure of him either. He's an enigma to us—just as, in some ways, we all are to each other.

It's interesting how he sometimes uses his cowl to find a level of consistency in himself. Push back the mask and Bruce Wayne seems lost and unsure. Slip it on and he becomes someone else, more confident in action, more definitive in deed. On the inside maybe Bruce Wayne is not that much removed from a little boy who lost his parents so very long ago. But Batman—the guy Bruce becomes when he's in costume—can't afford to express doubts or insecurity. His mask doesn't just hide his features: it helps define them.

Like Batman, all of us hide behind our masks and use them to help define ourselves for others. We all have secret identities of a sort, hidden behind our smiling social-networking profiles or our happy church faces. They're not lies, really. They're just not the whole truth, because we know that most of the people we encounter day-to-day couldn't handle the truth (or perhaps we couldn't handle giving it to them). Most of us are like those Russian nesting dolls, presenting a slightly different visage to the world depending on which world we're dealing with at the time. The outermost doll isn't a lie: mine still offers part of who I am, but it's not *all* of who I am. As I get closer to people, the nesting dolls open and the masks change. But it's a rare person whom I allow to see what's at my core: my innermost thoughts and fears, my dreams and desires, my pettiness and peevishness. Most of us know that if we threw ourselves open to the whole world, what would be revealed isn't always that attractive. It can be silly or ugly or off-putting, and so we only shed our masks a bit at a time.

The masks we wear aren't lies. They are, in a strange way, a critical part of who we are. Batman's not unusual in wearing one: his is just a little more obvious.

In Batman's case, though, it's harder to determine what his "mask" really is—and perhaps *he's* not even completely sure. He wears one when making the rounds in Gotham to bring down the bad guys. But there's another he wears, far more like the ones we show people at work or school or at the latest party: his Bruce Wayne mask, the playboy billionaire visage that he pastes on for dinners and charity balls. Lots of folks would argue that Bruce hides behind his perfectly coiffed hair and ever-easy smile far more than Batman does underneath his cowl.

In the ultra-creepy graphic novel *Arkham Asylum: A Serious House on Serious Earth*, the Dark Knight finds himself virtually imprisoned in Gotham City's most notorious locale for the criminally insane—at the mercy of the madmen he put there. Unconscious, Batman is momentarily helpless, and Arkham's inmates—led by Batman's personal demon, the Joker—can pretty much have their way with him.

"I say we take off his mask," says one loon in the gloom. "I want to see his *real* face."

"Oh, don't be so predictable!" Joker says. "That *is* his real face."

That's one of the interesting things about Gotham: it can be difficult to figure out just what constitutes a mask. It's not just Batman who wears one.

In *Batman Begins*, who is the real Dr. Crane: the apparently mild-mannered psychiatrist or the nightmare called Scarecrow? What's the true face of Two-Face in *The Dark Knight*? And what about the Joker's ghastly white face? Is that a mask? Is that who he truly is?

The answer to these questions may be yes, oddly enough. Gotham City is a place where masks reveal as much as they obscure—perhaps not unlike our own. And using this curiously paradoxical construct, it's satisfying to me that Joker's two most recent cinematic appearances give us two opposite, and yet somehow complementary, looks at his unforgettable visage.

In Tim Burton's 1989 film *Batman*, the Joker (played by Jack Nicholson) is literally a white-faced, green-haired freak, made that way through an unfortunate chemical accident. To appear more human, he must wear flesh-colored makeup. Nearly twenty years later, Christopher Nolan's Joker (Heath Ledger) in *The Dark Knight* achieves his trademark look *through* makeup—plastering his face with white greasepaint and dyeing his hair green. In the first version, Joker becomes a monster who hides behind a mask; in the second, he uses a mask not to hide but to reveal his true nature, his inner self. These opposing views of the clown's face point to a certain push-pull found in our own natures: how we can be corrupted both from without and within, how through practice we hide what we are, and how we become what we pretend to be.

All of which makes me wonder: if our souls had faces—if our souls *were* our faces—what would we look like?

## THE DARK OF THE KNIGHT

When my son, Colin, was about four years old, someone asked him if he was scared of the dark.

"No," he said thoughtfully. "It's the stuff *in* the dark I'm scared of."

We live in fear of the dark not because of what it is but because of what it hides. As children, we shone flashlights under our beds to dispel the creatures lurking there. As adults, we flick on lamps to better see where to walk, sit, or stand. We grow uncomfortable when we sit in the dark, surrounded by the unknown and unknowable.

Batman gets all that. In Gotham City, darkness is the refuge of monsters. It's the cover under which its thugs and thieves go to work, where gangsters and murderers and costumed villains come out to play. There's a lot to be scared of there, in the dark. And that is why Batman would tell you he's out there too: to give Gotham's worst something *they* should fear for a change. For crooks and criminals, *Batman* is what goes bump in the night.

But it's more than that. There's something inherently dark about Batman, too—something beyond his co-opting darkness for a lighter purpose or piecing together a mythos of fear to give evildoers something to be afraid of. Batman creators Bob Kane and Bill Finger imagined him in 1939 as a threatening, fearsome vigilante, despised by crooks and cops alike. And after so many years, he's never completely lost that sense of shadow. In Christopher Nolan's iteration of the character, that sense of darkness is as strong as ever. The films toy with the character's near-schizophrenic duality—his masks upon masks—and suggest at times that the gulf between the super-hero and the villains he fights isn't all that broad.

"Don't talk like one of them," the Joker tells Batman in *The Dark Knight*. "You're not, even if you'd like to be. To them, you're just a freak . . . like me!"

"What you really fear is inside yourself," Henri Ducard, a mentor of sorts to Bruce Wayne in *Batman Begins*, says. "You fear your own power. You fear your anger, the drive to do great or terrible things."

"It's the stuff *in* the dark I'm scared of," my son says.

Perhaps we're all a little like that. We fear the darkness inside ourselves. Our anger. Our jealousy. Our desires. Our hatred. I wonder sometimes if the reason why some of us hate to be still or alone is that in the quiet of our own thoughts we find ourselves facing the darkness within—unmasked, inconsistent with the person we wish to be. We may tell our-selves that we're "good people," kind and honest and decent. And most of the time it may be true. But in the darkness, we know—we *know*—that it's not. We know it's a mask.

And maybe that's one of the elements that attracts us to Batman.

In most superhero stories, the line between good and evil, the gulf between light and darkness, is clearly defined. On one side of the line you have the good guys, the caped wonders who protect innocent civilians from those on the opposite side, the evil ones, the villains, the ugly "other." It's us versus them, and there's no question that we're the guys wearing the white hats. There's something comforting about that narrative, which is a big reason why we see so many iterations of it.

But there's a part of us, maybe a small, nagging, unpleasant part, that treats those stories with suspicion. We know the line is not that bright; the gulf between "us" and "them" is not that wide. We feel not just the hero inside us but the villain . . . the darkness.

Batman, a guy who doesn't just wear a black hat, but one with pointed, horn-like ears, is a representation of our own selves, a strange, graphic allegory of the soul, with Gotham City a microcosm of the fragile, fallen world through which we struggle to make our way. Gotham itself feels *bad*—Old Testament bad. We can catch a glimpse of ancient Sodom or Samaria when we see its streets, and we feel its sin press on us with an almost physical presence. Batman, as we're told in *The Dark Knight*, isn't a perfect savior for the city; he's the one it "deserves," in all his imperfection. He walks perilously close to the line.

And yet there's something inside the guy that sets him apart. He may look bad, but it's not what he looks like that matters. It's what he does, and what he stands for, that counts.

How curiously biblical Batman is in this way. He's not much like Superman, but he is something like Moses, David, and Peter. The Bible doesn't sugarcoat our heroes for us or tell us they're anything but pretty sorry, flawed folks. And yet God takes them and makes them special, even great, just as he does with us. God takes badness and makes it good. He takes shadow and shines a light—if not on it, at least in it. He transforms us not from the outside, but from within.

Nothing is too sooty for his cleansing hand. "For once you were full of darkness, but now you have light from the Lord," says Ephesians 5:8. "So live as people of light!"

Is it surprising, then, that Batman would see some light and hope in Gotham as well? The place may be bad, filled with all manner of corruption, but there's goodness to be found underneath the grime. It isn't Sodom, without even ten righteous people. It can still be saved. It can still be redeemed—if only someone would care enough to help the cause along. Someone with a little faith.

## LOOKING FOR THE LIGHT

If you've been involved with Christianity for any length of time, you've met Christians who don't seem Christian at all. Maybe they raise their hands in church or say the right things in youth group, but you'd never know they were children of light by the way they behave outside of church.

But have you ever met atheists or agnostics or people who are thoroughly secular who didn't seem like they were following their *own* faith (or lack thereof) either?

I have. I've known people who say they don't believe in God—maybe even *can't* believe in him—but act as if they do. And they go beyond just generally adhering to Judeo-Christian ethics or throwing some walk-around money into the Salvation Army kettle at Christmas. There's nothing that says atheists who act like atheists can't also be nice, kind, and good people. But some I've met, it's as if they're following an unsounded call, as if they sense the hand of God on their shoulder but can't or won't give it a name.

It's a curious thing, but I think I understand it. God still loves us and cares for us even if we don't know him or love him back. Just because we shut our eyes to the light doesn't mean it leaves us or that we might not somehow see it a little, even against the walls of our eyelids.

"A man can no more diminish God's glory by refusing to worship Him than a lunatic can put out the sun by scribbling the word 'darkness' on the walls of his cell," writes C. S. Lewis in *The Problem of Pain*. "But God wills our good, and our good is to love Him . . . and to love Him we must know Him: and if we know Him, we shall in fact fall on our faces. If we do not, that only shows that what we are trying to love is not yet God—though it may be the nearest approximation to God which our thought and fantasy can attain."

Which makes me wonder whether Christians who don't act like Christians and unbelievers who act like they believe may be wandering down parallel roads on the way to faith. In both cases, they're craving to do what they were built to do; they want to worship, but they can't quite get there yet.

I think Batman is a little like that—either a nominal Christian who might not fully understand who he's following or a principled agnostic who somehow senses the call of God.

See, we don't really know what Batman believes. We don't see him go to church in the comics, and it seems unlikely he'd be the type to attend a Bible study. When the folks at Adherents.com tried to figure out what sort of faith various superheroes practiced, they concluded that Batman was probably a lapsed Catholic or disgruntled Episcopalian. DC author Chuck Dixon personally believes he's Catholic. "No Protestant ever suffered guilt the way Bruce does," Dixon writes. But Batman's not one to prattle on about his faith, and when the subject does come up, his response is often inconsistent.

Batman's faith is dependent on who might be telling his story that particular day. At times, he professes incredulity to the very concept of God, and given his dour practicality and stoic adherence to empirical evidence, that makes narrative sense. At other times, though, we see him praying. And when we think about the Dark Knight's unshakable sense of what's right and wrong, when we see his commitment to a justice that goes well beyond the law, and when we sometimes see manifested in him a curious and welcome form of grace, none of which seems consistent through a philosophy built around pragmatism and empiricism alone, a religious way of thinking also seems to fit. While Batman seems to have taken a more agnostic turn over the last several years, there's no getting around the fact that in the comics, Bruce might never have become Batman had he not bowed his head in the candlelight and prayed—a part of the Batman narrative we'll deal with at greater length in the next chapter.

As you read this book, I recommend you look at Batman not as a superhero saint, but rather as an unwitting guide. He's a creature of darkness in search of the light. He's no Messiah. He's not, perhaps, even a Christian. And yet when we watch him, there are unmistakable impulses within him that can have no other source than God—even if he or his authors don't fully understand that source. Who except one touched by God so fully acknowledges the darkness within himself? Who except one kissed by the Almighty rejects his own desires so thoroughly for the betterment of others? What idiot would sacrifice so much night after night without sensing a call?

Batman is no lunatic. He is no villain. He is a hero, pressed into service by a source he may be only dimly aware of. He believes in goodness even if he doesn't call it God. Perhaps he's like the disciple Thomas, who heard the call to follow, but didn't quite understand who he was really following.

But because Batman perhaps doesn't perfectly understand his calling or the implications thereof, he can sometimes get a little lost. He can grow confused in his role and sometimes his values can get a little scrambled. He is prone, like most of us can be at times, to place his trust in the wrong things and his faith in the wrong people. We all lose sight of God and sometimes chase after the nearest approximation. And sometimes he literally follows the wrong guy.

## "I BELIEVE IN HARVEY DENT"

In *The Dark Knight*, Bruce Wayne thinks he's found his savior—a crusading district attorney by the name of Harvey Dent.

"We all know you're Gotham's white knight," Jim Gordon tells Dent, and it would seem to be true. Winning the district attorney job behind the slogan "I Believe in Harvey Dent," he carries an explicit mandate to clean up the city. He plays by the rules in the light of day and does so in a coat and tie, not a cowl and cape. He's not afraid to show his face, and in the corrupted world of Gotham City, that makes Harvey a tough hombre indeed.

But if we've learned anything through Christopher Nolan's first two Gotham City sojourns, it's that there are few people on the public dole to be trusted. Every now and then we hear hints that perhaps Harvey's not as pure and virtuous as we've been led to believe. Jim Gordon lets slip that some cops have even given him a rather unfortunate nickname—"Harvey Two-Face," we learn later.

But Bruce Wayne doesn't see that side of the DA and takes Harvey at face value.

"You know that day that you once told me about, when Gotham would no longer need Batman?" he tells Rachel Dawes, his oldest friend and one of the few people who knows who's under the cowl. "It's coming. . . . It's happening now. Harvey is that hero. He locked up half of the city's criminals, and he did it without wearing a mask. Gotham needs a hero with a face."

We all need that hero, someone to protect us, to save us from our sinful world, from our sinful selves. Bruce Wayne knows that Batman—as tough and cool as he is—can't be that hero. He knows his own heart too well. And he, like the rest of Gotham, longs for someone without blemish, unstained by the muck and filth of the city. He doesn't seem to understand that even a good man or a great man is still also a *hu*man. Humans don't come without blemish. And sometimes our heroes let us down.

Listen to the language Batman uses when talking about Gotham's supposed white knight. Bruce Wayne didn't just grow to like Harvey Dent or decide to support Harvey Dent. "I *believe* in Harvey Dent," he says, echoing the DA's own slogan. He christens the politician as Gotham's duly elected savior, pinning the city's hopes—and his own—on Harvey's broad shoulders. Dent is cast as the city's messiah, a larger-than-life figure who will rescue Gotham from evil and turn it into a shining city on a hill.

But Harvey, as anyone who has seen *The Dark Knight* knows, is not an unspoiled Christ figure, incorruptible and pure. To paraphrase the Joker, he is only as good as circumstances allow him to be. Sure, Harvey says that he knew the risks . . . but he didn't know the half of it.

The Joker kidnaps Harvey and his main squeeze, Rachel Dawes, imprisoning them in gasoline-filled warehouses on opposite sides of town. But while Harvey's prepared to die, he's not prepared to live. So when Batman pulls him from the warehouse, with Rachel instead serving as the Joker's sacrificial lamb, something snaps. Harvey survives, grotesquely scarred on the inside and out, becoming the "Two-Face" his critics always said he was. He's no hero: he's as two-faced as the rest of us can be—a creature lost and alone and very, very angry. "It's not fair!" we can practically hear him say. "It doesn't make sense! What twisted, godforsaken world would allow this?" It's the stuff of Greek tragedy, and Harvey's fall, for all the millions the movie earned, makes *The Dark Knight* a hard film to watch.

"The Joker chose me!" Harvey hollers, the left side of his face charred and torn.

"Because you were the best of us," Batman tells him. "He wanted to prove that even someone as good as you could fall."

"And he was right," Harvey says.

I wonder if in that moment Batman feels Harvey's fall almost as keenly as Harvey does himself. After all, Batman believed in him. Bruce had wanted him to be the hero Gotham needed. But instead, Harvey Dent becomes a villain. Instead of a white knight, he's a killer, ugly, misshapen, unhinged from any strictures of normalcy or morality. Batman believed in Harvey, and when Harvey turned Two-Face, Batman's own hopes for a savior crumbled.

## POLEAXING THE PEDESTALS

I'd argue that no one deserves our full trust. As a species, we're just not that trustworthy. We look for saviors in people who, when push comes to shove, are in just as great a need of saving as we are.

We hear about fallen saviors every day of the week. Priests, politicians, and celebrities topple off the pillars we put them on in spectacular fashion, their sins and misdeeds spread across news and gossip sites for all the world to see and pass judgment. When I was a religion reporter in Colorado Springs, I had the opportunity to get to know dozens of spiritual leaders, and when I had to write about how some of them fell, maybe I felt a little of Batman's pain. These were people I liked and who were doing some great work in the community. But they had problems and issues, and those sins don't always stay hidden. Reactions to these fallen saviors were mixed, naturally. Some who followed these people decided to follow them still, denying most or all of what they were accused of. Others—often those standing on the outside—gleefully helped pull them down. Still others were heartbroken, their faith momentarily adrift: when the man who led you to God proves to be a hypocrite, it can understandably do funny things to your belief structure. If a pastor preaches fidelity and we find out he's having an affair, we can wonder whether the rest is also a big sham.

I reported on it all as fairly and objectively as I knew how. But inside, I hurt a little. And I remembered what my own pastor said in church one night: if a news crew showed up at the door of any of our souls, they'd find a juicy story there, too.

We've all been disappointed by those around us. We've all been disappointed in ourselves. We can be creatures of darkness, and when we find light in one another, it's often light of a flickering sort, prone to warble and wave with each gust of wind. So the light we see in even our heroes—even Batman—cannot be fully trusted. But holding mere candles in the darkness doesn't negate the sunlight overhead.

Batman chose the wrong savior—a corruptible DA, not the incorruptible Adonai. And yet he has not stopped believing. His faith in Harvey was misplaced, but he hasn't lost sight of the light Harvey reflected. He can't believe in Harvey Dent, but he can believe, as Harvey once did, that Gotham can be saved. And perhaps lodged somewhere in Batman's call, in his faith, in his desire for goodness and justice, there's a hint of the true Savior.

"The night is darkest just before the dawn," Harvey says before his fall. "And I promise you, the dawn is coming."

Batman lives in darkness. In some ways he is a creature of darkness. And like many of us, he can't quite get a handle on the coming sun. He's a little lost, a little alone, a little confused. And yet he has hope, and even faith of a sort—faith in a future that won't be corrupted, that won't be stained. He believes the dawn is coming . . . and that when it does, it will sweep away not just the city's shadows but his own.

Batman is on a walk of faith, following a voice to his ultimate purpose. His walk doesn't necessarily parallel our own, but it's instructive nonetheless. He is, like we are, following a worthy call—his to serve Gotham, ours to serve God and his people. And Batman shows us just how difficult and rewarding following that call can be.

When did Batman first hear that call? When did Bruce Wayne take his first steps toward his cape and cowl? It didn't come in earthquake or fire or even a still, small voice. It came with the tug of a trigger, the crack of a gun. It came with the sound of flight, the sound of a fall, the sound of an awful, deathly quiet. It came on the heels of a sob.

Turn the page and read on. It's time to learn how Batman was born.

## Chapter 2

# MARKED

*I didn't know how to name you then. But I see it
was you. Always you were calling me.*
—Jack in Terrence Malick's *The Tree of Life*

**BIRTH IS A VIOLENT THING.**

Life begins in agony and blood; a new soul finds voice in pain. And as we grow, that pain never seems to leave us—not entirely, anyway. Pain is always with us, and it's at its keenest in our most formative moments.

On a dark night in Gotham City, Batman was born.

Bruce Wayne was a child then, walking with his parents down a dark, dirty street in Gotham. Perhaps they were heading home after a movie or, as it is in *Batman Begins*, leaving an opera, dressed in black.

Out of the shadows steps a man, lean-eyed and hungry, holding a gun, demanding money. Something is said. Something goes wrong. Then a shot. And another. And Bruce's world is, from top to bottom, torn in two.

## WHISPERS

Christians sometimes talk about their "calling" with what seems to me amazing self-assurance. "God called me to be an actuary," a Christian might say, or, "I really felt God calling me to mow Mrs. McKenzie's lawn," or even, "I felt led to order a large Coke today."

I sometimes envy these folks—people who seem to know definitely what God wants from them in any given moment. They sound as though they and God have intimate, two-way chats over a venti mocha. Sometimes it makes me wonder if I'm doing something wrong—whether I'm simply not "Christian" enough to hear from God so clearly, so directly (or at least receive the occasional text message). *What an awesome bit of assurance to have*, I think . . . since I rarely have it. Most of the mammoth decisions I've made (and some pretty minor ones too) have been accompanied with much floor pacing, hand wringing, and Tylenol taking. I might wake up feeling absolutely sure of what the right course of action is and then change my mind entirely before the shower water heats up. Deciphering God's call is tricky business for me, even with dutiful prayer and quiet time. During my last job interview, for a Christian ministry, my future boss asked me if I felt "called" to work for them. "Maybe," I said with all the conviction such an indecisive word can muster. "Do you feel called to hire me?"

We can't look ahead as if our life were a comic book. We can't fast-forward it as we can a movie. Sometimes we don't seem to get much help from God in the moment. It's hard to know when we've been truly called by God for a special purpose—when we're being marked for his work.

Which might be one of the reasons why I find Bruce Wayne's transformation into Batman so compelling—and a little disturbing. His calling, like most of ours, was a long and gradual one, involving a strange brew of what seems like both chance and destiny, elements of faith and free will. And—here's the disturbing thing—pain and anguish were inescapable parts of it. It's an outlandish concoction, when you think about it, and one that culminates in an equally improbable outcome. But really it's not much more ludicrous than many of our lives, when it comes right down to it. We all know how much missed appointments and chance encounters weave themselves indelibly into our fabric—how we literally bumped into a future spouse at a coffee shop or found our life's purpose through a serendipitous Facebook post. We know, too, what an impact loss can have in our lives.

But even when our calling feels indistinct, I think it's there, insistent if not unmistakable. Sometimes it's revealed to us bit by bit, like a story or song. And sometimes, its beginnings take root in tragedy.

Batman was birthed through death. But his story doesn't begin there. It begins with Bruce Wayne himself—a carefree, perhaps pampered boy who had no idea what was in front of him.

## CALLED FROM BIRTH

Bruce was marked from birth, and so are we. "You made all the delicate, inner parts of my body," the psalmist writes in Psalm 139:13, "and knit me together in my mother's womb." Some of our talents, inclinations, and personality traits are hardwired into our DNA by God for a future we couldn't possibly envision. Like a sculptor eyeing a raw piece of marble, God had an idea of what he wanted to create with us from the get-go, and he gives us certain gifts that might help make his plan a reality.

Sometimes those gifts seem obvious—talent so outrageously outsized it seems almost unfair. When Mozart started cranking out musical compositions at age five, it became pretty evident that the kid was meant to be a composer. When tennis phenom Andre Agassi started whupping some pretty decent adult tennis players when he was nine, observers had little doubt he'd make his mark as a pro.

And while some folks might point to such outlandish abilities as proof of God's divine blessing (and really, they'd be right), it's interesting to me that these gifts can seem less like a gift and more like a hindrance. Mozart died nearly alone (and quite unhappily, some suggest) at the age of thirty-five. And while Agassi eventually did become a fantastic tennis player and a good all-around human being, he hated tennis for years before finding a level of peace with the game. Even heroes from the Bible—overtly blessed by God with some pretty amazing abilities—had their struggles. Take Samson, the Israelite judge with superhuman strength. He got carried away with himself and spent his last days as a prisoner with his eyes gouged out, according to Judges 16. Or consider Joseph, who was given great abilities to interpret dreams and manage others' affairs, but who was given a cushy job only after his brothers sold him into slavery.

So while God uses people with out-of-this-world skill

sets, he reserves his most noteworthy jobs for people of more modest means, those whose talents aren't fully realized until they're progressively shaped for God's purposes. Many of our biblical heroes weren't kings or philosophers from powerful nations but shepherds and fishermen eking out a living on a dry, dusty spit of land stretched lengthwise near the Mediterranean Sea. Had God not specifically marked Moses or Samuel or Peter for his work, they would have lived and died in obscurity, lost to spiritual and national history alike. It was God's call that made them important, not their own superlative abilities.

God likes to make use of us average Joes and Janes—or, since hardly anyone's named Joe or Jane these days, average Jacobs and Isabellas. Which, when you think about it, sounds an awful lot like Batman.

*What?* I can hear you say. *Batman an average Joe? C'mon! Does the whole "World's Greatest Detective" moniker not mean anything to you? Or the fact that he repeatedly beats up Killer Croc with his bare hands?*

And if you did speak to me in all italics like that, you'd have a point. While Batman doesn't have awesome, outlandish powers like most of his superhero buds, he's considerably stronger and smarter than the average billionaire playboy. He could probably turn some heads at the NFL combine in the morning, then snag some cash during a *Jeopardy!* taping that evening.

But his gifts took time to develop, and he developed them only after he began to see the purpose for which he had been made. There's nothing I've seen, in either the comics or the movies, that suggests Bruce Wayne was a prodigy—a freak of nature, blessed with jaw-dropping strength or a dizzying natural intellect. From what we see and read, Bruce was a normal, albeit rich, kid. We couldn't say for sure whether he was a good student or a promising basketball player or a dynamite saxophonist. Indeed, the young Bruce Wayne looks, if anything, a little more pensive in *Batman Begins* than the typical rough-and-tumble lad—more nerd than jock, more marching band than football team. He's thin and thoughtful . . . and his best friend is a girl, Rachel Dawes, at an age when most boys know that girls are at the very least lame and at worst cootie carriers. When his parents take him to an opera, the sight of dancers dressed in creepy bat costumes freaks him out so much that he begs his father to take him home.

Bruce, something special? Not so much. Unless, of course, you're talking about what his father and mother think. To them Bruce was very special indeed. And through them something *truly* special began to take root.

## THE LOVE OF A FATHER

From *Batman Begins* we know that Bruce's father, Thomas, was an engaged and attentive parent and did his best to instill a sense of character in the boy. Bruce knew his father was a doctor and that he took care of the sick. Bruce knew his father was rich but that he didn't lavish his wealth solely on himself. In the midst of Gotham's crushing depression, Thomas Wayne built a public transportation system to "unite the city" and alleviate some of its economic woes. And when

Bruce fell down into a dark, scary cave filled with bats—a moment that would first haunt, then inspire him—it was his father, not a servant, who came to his rescue, turning even that near tragedy into a teachable moment.

"We took quite a fall, didn't we, Master Bruce?" says the faithful family butler, Alfred.

"And why do we fall, Bruce?" Thomas says, carrying the boy into the house. "So we can learn to pick ourselves up."

The lessons clearly took. Before Bruce was marked by tragedy, his father had marked the boy with love. Thomas Wayne, the first hero Bruce ever knew, taught him that heroes are more than strong; they're compassionate. They're not invincible, just resilient. These are lessons Bruce never forgot—and he never forgot who taught them to him.

"You're stronger than your father," Henri Ducard, Bruce's mentor, tells him many years later.

"You didn't know my father," Bruce answers.

We're all given certain talents and taught certain lessons throughout our lives. Some of these lessons are intentionally taught to us; others are lessons we've been indirectly exposed to, watching the way people act or respond. They're all part of our fabric, absolutely instrumental in who we are and who we're becoming. Sometimes these lessons are not altogether positive. Sometimes we have to overcome what we've been taught in order to be the people God wants us to be. But thankfully for Bruce Wayne, his dad taught him good lessons, critical lessons. Through Bruce's father, God marked Bruce to transcend being just another tortured soul scarred by circumstance. Thomas had given him the tools he needed to deal with that fateful night of tragedy and death.

But that didn't make those terrible events—or the years that followed—any easier to stomach.

## UNWANTED CALL

The superhero origin story is almost always tinged by tragedy. Spider-Man loses his uncle, the Hulk loses part of his humanity, Superman loses his whole home world. But a spiritual thread runs through each of these tragedies, bearing just a hint of Christianity's Easter story: out of death comes life; out of an end, a new beginning.

But even while this sense of paradox—that death and sacrifice can somehow bring about new life and redemption—is at the absolute center of the Christian faith, it's still a hard concept for lots of Christians, including me, to fully grasp. It's kind of a horrible thought to think that Thomas and Martha Wayne's deaths were somehow meant to be, isn't it? That God chose to mark a little boy for special work by killing his parents? It doesn't sit well with us. The concept of an all-powerful, deeply merciful God *allowing* us to suffer, to experience seemingly senseless pain, is problematic enough. It's a lot more difficult to figure this pain might somehow be part of his plan.

If Bruce Wayne were a religious man, this is a question he might ponder from time to time as he changes into his cape and cowl and dashes to the Batmobile—how different his life might have been had his parents lived that night. What might have happened had they watched him grow up?

Would he be a doctor? A lawyer? Would he have a wife? Children? Surely he wouldn't be gallivanting in the dead of night in a black mask and tights, would he?

What would have happened had Bruce Wayne, on that night, not been marked?

## CALLED THROUGH TRAGEDY

I wonder how long Bruce waited there in the shadows for the police to arrive. A minute? An hour? We can't know from the comics or the movies. We see the moment of loss in one panel or scene. In the next, we're whisked away, spared from witnessing Bruce watch as his parents grew cold. And so I wonder, what did he do? Did he try to hold them in his arms, as they had held him? Did he scream for help? Did he sit, terrified, in silence? When did he know they were gone? When did Bruce Wayne fully understand that his father—his hero—had been taken from him?

"My God, my God, why have you abandoned me?" the psalmist cries (Psalm 22:1)—a cry echoed by Jesus himself as he hung on the cross. Maybe Bruce said something much like this as he felt his parents slip away.

Sometimes the horror we feel in the midst of life's tragedies cannot be reconciled with an all-good, all-knowing God. Sometimes I think we do God a disservice when we talk about his "master plan," even though I believe he has one. The terminology, in our finite minds, suggests that everything that happens in our lives is done by divine writ, and considering how many awful things we endure, that can make God look pretty mean-spirited. Your dog was hit by a car? God willed it. Someone broke into your house? God ordered that up too. Sickness, suicide, murder—how could a good God cause such things to happen? How could he allow it?

In the book of Job, the titular character loses everything: his wealth, his family, his health. Job's friends assume the guy deserved it, that Job's tribulations were caused by God himself: "This was the home of a wicked person," says Job's friend Bildad, "the place of one who rejected God" (Job 18:21). And when God finally answers Job about why he has received such shoddy treatment, he says, in no uncertain terms (and with blistering sarcasm), that it's not Job's place to ask: humans don't have the wherewithal to grasp the answer.

"Where were you when I laid the foundations of the earth?" God thunders. "Tell me, if you know so much. Who determined its dimensions?" (Job 38:4-5).

Through God's response, Job learned that the "why" of it all was, perhaps, beside the point. The thing that mattered was not the "why" but the "what next"—how he responded to the trials set before him.

I'm no theologian. There are lots of folks who have spent far more time contemplating the problem of pain and how it can coincide with an all-powerful, deeply loving God. But I don't think God *makes* people suffer through other people's sin—which is the root of much of the pain we experience in this world. I don't believe God *made* Joseph's brothers toss the poor kid down a well or *made* Judas betray his Son. I don't believe God would have *made* Joe Chill shoot Bruce Wayne's parents, either. Those marks have another root source.

But while God may not *cause* that sort of trauma, I firmly believe he can work through it. "You intended to harm me," Joseph tells his brothers, "but God intended it all for good. He brought me to this position so I could save the lives of many people" (Genesis 50:20). God is, among everything else, the master of the impossible ninth-inning comeback, author of the jaw-dropping twist in the story. God loves paradox, which perhaps explains why his greatest work was done in the midst of the seeming catastrophe of his own Son's death.

"When Judas sinned, Jesus paid," writes Dorothy Sayers in *Letters to a Diminished Church.* "He brought good out of evil, He led out triumph from the gates of Hell and brought all mankind out with him; but the suffering of Jesus and the sin of Judas remain a reality. God did not abolish the fact of evil: He transformed it. He did not stop the Crucifixion: He rose from the dead."

We see a hint of this paradox in the dark and terrible alley-way where Bruce sits with his lifeless parents. As he waits for help to come too late, the reality slowly rakes its claws against the boy's psyche, leaving horrible scars—marks that will last a lifetime. Sometimes people who suffer such scars never recover. Sometimes such wounds destroy their victims, one way or another, and perhaps they might have destroyed Bruce Wayne, too.

But underneath those marks is written something more: a purpose. We saw earlier that in life, Bruce's father had given him the tools to become a hero. In his death, he gave Bruce a reason to use them.

"My God, my God, why have you abandoned me?" Jesus

cried on the cross (Matthew 27:46). To some this might suggest doubt—a strange emotion, one would think, for the Son of God. But Jesus knew his Scripture. He knew the rest of the psalm—a powerful prayer that swings from terrible fear to unwavering faith:

> Yet you brought me safely from my mother's womb
>> and led me to trust you at my mother's breast.
> I was thrust into your arms at my birth.
>> You have been my God from the moment I was born.
> Do not stay so far from me,
>> for trouble is near,
>> and no one else can help me.
>
> PSALM 22:9-11

Job heard God without mistake. But for the psalmist, like most of us, God's voice is not as clear. Sometimes God does not speak in the midst of pain. He offers no answers. And yet the psalmist's answer is much the same as Job's: to be thankful, to trust, to serve.

"My God, my God, why?" This question marked the end of Jesus' life. When we utter the same cry, we're often simply at a crossroads—a place in time where we've been marked, definitely by life and perhaps by God. When we put aside the "why" and push on with the challenges that lie before us, that's often when we can see the path God has set in front of us better—see with more clarity the role he has in mind for us. The pain sharpens us, molds us . . . and sometimes forces us to become more than what we are.

The pain marked the beginning of a new life for Bruce Wayne. His path was narrowing. With his parents' death, he had the driving force to become a hero. With his father's teaching, he had the heart. But was his path to becoming Batman thus inevitable? Had Bruce's destiny been set? Was he ready to order a cape, stock his utility belt, and get to it?

## CALLED THROUGH SEARCHING

God doesn't rush—much to our chagrin. We're impatient creatures with a fondness for fast cars, fast food, microwave ovens, and credit cards. We don't like waiting, which means, if we're honest with ourselves, our relationship with God sometimes feels strained. For us, an hour is an eternity. For God, eternity is an hour. He marks us for a lifetime of service, but he sometimes makes us wait for decades to learn what that service might be. It took Joseph years to move from the bottom of that well to his chosen place of power in Egypt, where he was able to rescue his brothers. Moses was an old man before God chatted with him through a burning bush. Even when we know God's plan, it takes time. David was anointed Israel's future king long before he took the crown: it took years—decades, in fact—and David spent his days killing giants, playing harps, leading armies, and running away from Israel's current king before circumstances were ready for him to claim the throne. And frankly, some folks close to David might have had their doubts whether the guy would get a chance at all.

In Batman's first origin story published in November 1939 ("The Batman Wars against the Dirigible of Doom" in

*Detective Comics* No. 33), Bruce finds his path pretty quickly after his parents' passing. In one panel we see Bruce, tears streaming down his face, saying, "Dead! They're d . . . dead." In the next, just "days later" according to the narration, he's at his bedside, praying by candlelight, "And I swear by the spirits of my parents to avenge their deaths by spending the rest of my life warring on all criminals." And then we see a grown-up Bruce fiddling with test tubes, lifting weights, and wondering what in the world to call his alter ego.

For most of us, the trek from pain to purpose isn't nearly as seamless as a two-panel transition. It takes most of us time to simply recover from life's big blows, and still more to move forward. Sometimes it takes tremendous courage to move on at all.

In *Batman Begins*, Bruce Wayne doesn't find his purpose as a child beside his bed. In fact, he begins his adult life lost, spiritually adrift. We learn that after his parents died, Bruce went to Princeton University but couldn't make it work.

"You don't like it there?" Alfred asks.

"I like it fine . . . they just don't feel the same way," Bruce answers.

So with college out of the picture, Bruce returns home, but he can't feel at home even there. He steers clear of the master suite, electing to sleep in the room he called his own as a child—symbolic, the film seems to suggest, of the fact that Bruce isn't yet willing to grow up. He may look like an adult, but he's still a child, unable to either give up his parents' memory or come to peace with their passing.

"This place is a mausoleum," he grumbles. "If I have my way, I'll pull the . . . thing down, brick by brick."

Thomas Wayne's lessons still linger under the surface. But Bruce, for the moment, pays them no mind. He has just one purpose now: to kill a killer and avenge his parents' death. But he never gets the chance. Before he can pull the trigger and put Joe Chill down for good, someone else beats him to it—a kamikaze assassin who works for Carmine Falcone, Gotham's biggest crime lord. Falcone, Bruce is told, created the conditions that made Joe Chill. Falcone was an instrument in his parents' death, Bruce believes. And now Falcone has taken away the only thing Bruce had left: vengeance.

But when Bruce confronts Falcone in a sleazy bar, Falcone gives the kid something he's never had before: motivation.

"Now, you think because your mommy and your daddy got shot, you know about the ugly side of life, but you don't," Falcone tells the furious boy. "You've never tasted desperate. You're Bruce Wayne, the Prince of Gotham; you'd have to go a thousand miles to meet someone who didn't know your name. So don't come down here with your anger, trying to prove something to yourself. This is a world you'll never understand. And you always fear what you don't understand."

Bruce leaves the bar and leaves Gotham, going a thousand miles and more, where no one knows his name. His purpose is to understand what he fears—to fall and get back up, again and again and again. He becomes a vagabond, living a hand-to-mouth existence in the farthest reaches of the globe. It's at this time that the youth—still not far removed from the time he begged his father to leave an opera because of the scary costumes—begins to train in earnest, though for what he's not quite sure. His mind and body become strong and formidable, but his purpose remains unclear until he's discovered by a man calling himself Henri Ducard, who offers to give Bruce direction and purpose. He hopes to craft the boy in his own image, to cause Bruce to look within himself and discover his true calling.

"If you make yourself more than just a man, if you devote yourself to an ideal, you become something else entirely," Ducard says. "Are you ready to begin?"

## CALLED BY CHOICE

Batman has many fathers in *Batman Begins*—many people who help shape and form this Caped Crusader. Thomas Wayne gives him the moral underpinnings; Joe Chill gives him the painful catalyst; Falcone sends him off for a hard-earned education. Ducard is there to pull all the elements together and create—much to Ducard's ultimate chagrin—a shadowy ideal. He asks Bruce to put aside what he is and become something greater than himself.

Anyone who's seen *Batman Begins* knows that Ducard is a little extreme in his views. But in truth, Ducard's core call here is very much like a biblical one.

"Follow me," Jesus said, and he wasn't just talking about tagging along with him down to the dock. Jesus asked (and asks) his disciples to set aside what they were and embrace something entirely new and different. He asked his followers to leave behind their old lives and often their livelihoods and set off on a new, uncertain adventure. The disciples were no longer merely individuals: they belonged to something greater. The New Testament is littered with exhortations for Christians to die to themselves and be transformed into new beings altogether—to be born again (see, for example, Matthew 16:24; John 3:3; Romans 12:2; Galatians 2:20). Jesus' literal call is not something to be taken on a whim. This is life-altering stuff. To follow Jesus means being marked for his purposes forever.

Ducard's League of Shadows, run by the über-shadowy Ra's al Ghul, demands the same sort of commitment. It seems unlikely that the men who join this league sign up for six months or so, punching a clock at the end of the working day before heading home to the wife and kids. The League demands everything from its followers—their bodies, minds, and souls. Ducard offers Bruce what he seems to want and need the most: a sense of purpose.

And all Bruce has to do to get it is sacrifice his past and his future.

He has to, in a sense, die to himself and become a weapon for unflinching justice. Like Jesus' movement nearly two millennia ago, the League, to Ducard, is a life-changing, world-changing force for good, an army capable of shaking society to its very core. It is Christianity without the love and mercy of Christ: an Old Testament–like sword of judgment capable of laying waste to whole lands. And Bruce, his parents' death still haunting him, seems the ideal weapon of vengeance.

Bruce trains with Ducard and the League for weeks,

months, perhaps even years. Through their tutelage, he transforms himself from a formidable, angry man-child to a finely honed weapon of muscle, bone, and brain. Finally he's ready to claim his place among the League's leaders: he passes a final test, bests his tutor Ducard, and stands before Ra's al Ghul, apparently ready to perform his last rite of initiation.

"We have purged your fear," Ducard intones. "You are ready to lead these men. You are ready to become a member of the League of Shadows. But first, you must demonstrate your commitment to justice."

Bruce watches as a man he knows as a thief and murderer is dragged into the chamber. He's a helpless captive, and Ducard holds out a sword for Bruce to take.

Bruce Wayne has come a long way from the time he had crouched in that dark street with his parents. He has traveled thousands of miles, lived a handful of hard years, suffered a hundred marks that all became integral to his calling. Thanks to al Ghul's League of Shadows, he has learned to fight, think on his feet, and "disappear." He has learned the value of theatricality and the importance of becoming more than a man. His parents' death left him with a strong desire to fight and throttle evil wherever he might find it. Now he is ready to answer his calling—to do what his years and experiences molded him to do.

But a calling isn't a matter of destiny, a duty God pushes us into. It requires from us a choice, a realization of the free will we've been given. Bruce has been pushed around by circumstances for years now, and every choice he has made has been to find salve for his pain, to find an answer for his suffering. Some of the choices have been hard, but they've been instinctive and almost entirely selfish, choices he knew he had to make to try to squelch his heartache.

Now Bruce comes upon a different sort of choice—a choice not to get something, but to give something. Every step he has made on his journey, both physical and spiritual, has led him here. For the Bruce we see in *Batman Begins*, that choice is nearly upon him.

Bruce shakes his head. "I'm no executioner," he says.

"Your compassion is a weakness your enemies will not share," Ducard tells him.

"That's why it's so important," Bruce answers. "It separates us from them."

In that moment, Bruce knows the sort of man he is and the sort of man he wants to be. Bruce finds purpose—rooted not in anger or sorrow, but in the gentle lessons taught by his father so many years before.

"It's not who you are underneath," Rachel tells Bruce in *Batman Begins*. "It's what you do that defines you." Bruce knows this as well as anyone. He's more than a collection of marks and scars accumulated through life. He's greater than his training. It's all part of who he is. But in the end, it's what he decides to do with all these marks that matters most.

Batman may have been born that dark night in a Gotham street. He was, in a sense, born again that day on the mountaintop, sword in fist, a life in his hands. He did not—could not— choose the circumstances of his becoming. None of us can. But we can choose what we do with those circumstances. We can choose to follow God's call. We can all choose to acknowledge his mark upon us.

While we sometimes think of this choice as a one-time thing, it's not. We choose to follow every day, every hour.

But following this call is never easy. Bruce's rejection of the sword on the top of that cold mountaintop led to a harrowing battle with the entire League of Shadows that Bruce barely survived—just the first of countless near-death experiences he'd suffer for his choice.

When we find our purpose and embrace what we were made for, things don't necessarily get easier. Very often they get harder. When we decide to stand for something, the shadowy line between "us" and "them" that we talked about in the last chapter gets a lot more obvious to us *and* to them, and the forces on the other side of that line seem to redouble their efforts to drag us across it. We struggle with sins and temptations, we find ourselves warring against the chaos and corruption all around us. When we follow Batman's example and choose to be heroes, our own weaknesses and the world's flaws hammer at us like never before. Sometimes they're subtle, barely discernible. Sometimes they're obvious threats to us or to others. And sometimes they greet us with a great big smile, a ghoulish laugh, and an invitation to hell.

## Chapter 3

# NEMESES

*Thus wrapped in mist*
*Of midnight vapour, glide obscure, and pry*
*In every bush and brake, where hap may find*
*The Serpent sleeping, in whose mazy folds*
*To hide me, and the dark intent I bring.*
—John Milton, *Paradise Lost*

## HEADS OR TAILS?

It's a question probably all of us have asked a time or two. When intellect and logic and emotion and persuasion fail us, we resort to fate—a two-sided coin we fling into the air and watch land. We flip when we're trying to decide whether to eat Mexican or Chinese for dinner. We flip for who's going to sleep on the top bunk. Sometimes if I'm in the mood for a candy bar (but know I shouldn't eat one), I'll fish out a coin and flip: Heads, I make my way down to the vending machine to buy a Butterfinger. Tails . . . well, I flip again. It's weird, I know, but if the coin tells me it's okay to consume a little chocolaty goodness, it must be better for me somehow.

But few of us take the flip of a coin as seriously as Two-Face.

For much of his life (we're told in *The Dark Knight*), Two-Face has carried a special two-headed coin his father gave him. In better days, when Two-Face was the charmed and charming Harvey Dent (the dapper DA Bruce Wayne once thought might be Gotham's savior), the coin was a sort of talisman, one he'd flip when making a decision he'd already made. But after being disfigured in a horrible, soul-scarring explosion, he found that his coin—one side, at any rate— had been scratched and blackened too . . . a cosmic joke on poor, tragic Dent. The coin became his conscience.

In a place filled with as much duality as Gotham City, Two-Face's coin makes for a pretty excellent illustration to flip around in our minds a little. As we've already seen, Two-Face isn't the only guy in town who seems to have dual identities. Bruce Wayne and Batman could be seen as two sides of the same coin—one dark, the other light (though which is which might take a graduate degree to piece together). Even if we set aside Bruce Wayne for a moment and look at the Caped Crusader, we see a hint of the coin: the superhero on a quest for justice and the brooding wraith who may be looking to salve his own pain.

Gotham itself has some serious duality going on, what with its crooked cops and principled vigilantes. And we could also look at Gotham as the flip side of our own world— a blackened, mottled facsimile of our own communities. Nearly everything we encounter in this imaginary world can be seen as a weird mimicry of our own—very different sides of a common coin. But maybe looking at Gotham is more like looking *through* the coin—almost as if it were Alice's looking glass or a funhouse mirror—to see the uncanny world beyond, both disturbingly strange and deeply familiar. It's a place of paradox, a world turned wrongways in which the bad guys sometimes wear badges, the good guys wear black, and clowns are never, ever funny.

All of this makes it a place in which Christians should be pretty comfortable. Our whole faith is rooted in paradox. Jesus tells us that we're strongest when we're weak, still loved by God when we're the least lovable. It's probably not necessary to point out that Christianity's greatest story—the story of Jesus—is utterly rife with paradox: a king born in a manger; a God who is a man; a Savior who doesn't save himself; a victory won through death and defeat.

Even when we look at our failings, they're often warped reflections of God's best gifts to us. The great Christian theologian Augustine tells us that "there is no possible source of evil except good," and in my experience that appears to be true. Every evil we commit is a corruption of something good and honorable in us. If we did not love, we could not lust. If we did not appreciate God's creation, we wouldn't be tempted by envy or gluttony. When we sin, we look upon God's goodness through a warped mirror. Our sins are the scarred side of a once-beautiful coin.

So it's hardly surprising that Batman's gallery of rogues—arguably the most formidable collection of baddies to ever be drawn in the world of comics—are often curious reflections of Batman's own being. And frankly, they're often perversions of who we are (or who we could be) too. And so in a way, just as they attack Batman with guns or knives or poison gas, they play havoc with our own lives. They represent obstacles we all have to face as Christians. They're our trials and temptations, our fears and sins. They're distortions of our best instincts, the flip sides of our better natures. And they can mess with us something awful.

While Batman has faced countless compelling villains during his long career in comics, television, and film—from the Penguin to the Man-Bat to the Mad Hatter—we must draw a line somewhere. We can't deal with every do-badder the Dark Knight has crossed metaphorical swords with. So with all due respect to the Riddler and Poison Ivy and Clayface, we're going to focus only on the primary evildoers found in Christopher Nolan's Batman trilogy. And as such, we should start with the first criminal we meet in Batman's origin story, *Batman Begins*.

## CARMINE FALCONE: CORRUPTION AND COMPROMISE

As we've seen, Falcone worms his way into Bruce Wayne's life long before he ever straps on a cape. The two meet in a seedy club, and Falcone advises the kid to leave. Quickly.

"Look around you," the mobster says. "You'll see two councilmen, a union official, a couple off-duty cops, and a judge." Then Falcone leans forward, pointing a gun at Bruce's chest. "Now, I wouldn't have a second's hesitation of blowing your head off right here and right now in front of 'em."

And Falcone, we sense, doesn't joke around. Clearly the mob boss is a bad, bad man.

He looks a lot different in the comics. In Batman's printed

works (most notably *The Long Halloween* saga of 1996–1997), the character's look and personality is largely based on Don Vito Corleone from *The Godfather*, with his nickname being The Roman. In *Batman Begins*, he's been stripped of his dapper tuxedo and pencil-thin mustache, but he still influences every corner of the city, playing ventriloquist to his puppets in government and law enforcement. It takes a brave man to stand up to Falcone's complicated network of deception. Or sometimes a strong woman.

"You care about justice?" Bruce's best friend, Rachel Dawes, asks him. "Look beyond your own pain, Bruce. This city is rotting. They talk about the Depression as if it's history, and it's not. Things are worse than ever down here. Falcone floods our streets with crime and drugs, preying on the desperate, creating new Joe Chills every day. Now, Falcone may've not killed your parents, Bruce, but he's destroying everything that they stood for."

Falcone rules the city through bribery, subterfuge, and fear. And he has Gotham's leaders sitting snugly in his pocket.

Falcone's corruption is an illustration of Augustine's theory of evil—something good turning into something else through taint and decay. Just as a nice quilt can be eaten by moths or a plump apple consumed by a worm, so Falcone nibbles away at Gotham's societal fabric, spoiling the whole thing bit by bit. You don't see Falcone challenging Gotham's few clean cops to a climactic duel à la the traditional supervillain. Falcone (much like sneaky sin itself) is way too smart and subtle for that. Why risk a face-to-face confrontation when it's so much easier, and so much more effective, to eat away from the inside?

But let's not lay too much blame at the feet of poor Falcone just yet. After all, you can't give someone a bribe if they're not willing to take it.

I live in Colorado, where we've been dealing with a practically apocalyptic attack of mountain pine beetles for a few years now. For those of you who aren't familiar with the critters, they essentially burrow into a variety of evergreen trees, lay eggs, and introduce a sap-stopping fungus into the tree's innards. Except for some telltale entrance wounds, infested trees look pretty green for a year after the infestation begins, so when they start looking sickly—their needles turning a disturbing reddish-brown—the pine beetle babies have already hatched and have set up shop in a different batch of trees.

But here's the thing: if a tree is already healthy, it stands a far better chance of beating off the advancing pine-beetle scourge.

Falcone's style of corruption feels a lot like a pine beetle infestation. Healthy communities are better able to resist the Falcones of the world. Unfortunately, Gotham wasn't particularly healthy. And so Falcone and other gangsters were able to make the place weaker and weaker until it was half dead, almost completely unable to defend itself.

But like the mostly green tree, the initial weaknesses that allowed Falcone access probably weren't seen as being very serious. Most folks probably didn't think they were doing anything wrong—or, at least, seriously wrong—when they first started taking money from the boss. Maybe they needed some extra cash for college or gambling debts or an operation. Maybe Falcone offered a big check for a small, seemingly innocuous job. It probably didn't seem like a big deal at the time. No harm, no foul, right? Taking a little money on the side doesn't mean you're a bad person, does it? It's just one step off the path, one little compromise. And compromise isn't all bad, is it?

No, it's not all bad. Compromise, strictly defined, can be right as rain. In its purest form, compromise means setting aside your own desires for someone else's with the understanding that they'll do the same for you. Most of us, whether we admit it or not, compromise a lot: we pick our battles, share our toys, and settle for half a loaf. The ability to compromise is critical for a healthy marriage and solid friendships. Without compromise, we'd be fighting with everyone all the time.

But when Falcone asks Gotham to compromise, it's a different thing altogether. When we make an honorable bargain, we give up something we want and feel better for it. When Falcone asks for a deal, we *get* something we want and feel worse. In the former, we compromise over something; in the latter, we compromise ourselves. We sell our values for a bit of silver, our souls in a Faustian deal.

Deep down, we know this sort of compromise is wrong, which is why it's invariably done in the dark. And Falcone, for his part, sees less daylight than Dracula. He does his business in shady nightclubs or shadowed piers, knowing the sorts of deals he cuts require the blanket of night. The apostle Paul cautions us to stay away from Falcone and his ilk. "Take no part in the worthless deeds of evil and darkness," he tells us in Ephesians 5:11-13. "Instead, expose them. It is shameful even to talk about the things that ungodly people do in secret. But their evil intentions will be exposed when the light shines on them."

Batman, by design or chance, takes care of Falcone in a particularly Pauline fashion. When he finally captures Falcone and leaves the mobster for the police to find, he straps him to a shining spotlight. Falcone is exposed, literally and metaphorically, by light.

## SCARECROW: FEAR

After Falcone is taken into custody, he tries to feign insanity—hoping to get a buy-in from Arkham Asylum's Dr. Jonathan Crane, a creepy psychiatrist with a penchant for the dramatic.

"Yeah, Doctor Crane, I can't take it anymore," he says with a virtual wink and nudge. "It's all too much. The walls are closing in. Blah, blah, blah." And then Falcone begins to cut yet another deal, working his powers of corruption and compromise on the good doctor: "I know you're planning something," he essentially tells him. "I can spoil your plans. Cut me in, and I'll let you go forward."

But rather than taking the bait, Crane sighs heavily and takes out a grotesque mask. "I use it in my experiments," he tells the puzzled Falcone. "Probably not very frightening to a guy like you, but these crazies, they can't stand it."

Crane puts the mask on and blows a powerful hallucinogen into Falcone's face. And the man who ruled Gotham for decades, the man who never knew fear no matter what sort of alleys he walked down, begins to scream.

Crane, otherwise known as Scarecrow, is a dealer in fear.

Again, we see a virtue (or at least a God-given instinct) twisted here. While our culture tells us that it's great to be fearless—we have everything from the X Games to an apparel company branded No Fear—you wouldn't be around to read this book if you took the culture at its word. There are lots of things we *should* be afraid of, from clogged arteries to the rabid dog down the street. A healthy fear of fire keeps you from sticking your hand in the flame to rescue that marshmallow for your s'more. A healthy fear of your boss keeps you from falling asleep at work. Fear keeps us prudent, keeps us safe, and sometimes keeps us on the straight and narrow. You're less likely to speed if you have a healthy fear of the highway patrol. You're more likely to eat your carrots if you have a healthy fear of your mother.

Fear is even biblical: "Let the whole world fear the Lord," reads Psalm 33:8, "and let everyone stand in awe of him." More than sixty passages exhort us to hold a healthy fear of the one who created us. Some Christians interpret this sort of fear to be more a sense of awe and wonder than terror. But if we turned a street corner and ran smack-dab into God . . . well, the meeting probably would leave us shaking in our wingtips.

Batman taps into that sense of good fear. His whole persona is crafted to stoke that fear in the right folks. "Bats frighten me," Bruce Wayne admits. "It's time my enemies shared my dread." And bad guys *should* be scared of Batman. This fear might encourage them to become a little better. The only way a thug can keep Batman off his case is to stop being so thuggish—stop terrorizing people and get a real job.

Scarecrow's fear is less constructive.

While a fear of God helps make us better people, there's another sort of fear that makes us worse. It's the fear of death, of pain, of shame. It's the stuff of nightmares or the things that go bump in the night. It's often (but not always) irrational, and while it has you in its grasp, it's overpowering. It's the sort of fear that turns us selfish and makes us cowards. When we're afraid like this, when we're in the grip of terror, we're worse than useless: we can be dangerous. Just ask any lifeguard what it's like to save a panicked, drowning man, and you'll hear just how dangerous fear can be.

"There's nothing to fear but fear itself!" Scarecrow shouts while mounted on a horse in *Batman Begins*, looking for all the world like Washington Irving's headless horseman. And in this case, he's right. Scarecrow fosters not just fright, but insanity. If a fear of Batman helps keep society in line, Scarecrow's sort of fear rips it off its hinges. Even Batman himself is not immune. Scarecrow's fear infects him, too. And that's significant, I think. We learn that no one can escape fear. A true hero simply acts in spite of it. A true hero masters his fear so it doesn't master him. And Batman does exactly that in *Batman Begins* with a little help from his friends and a hastily concocted antidote.

The threat isn't over, though. Fear isn't just a state of being; it's a weapon manufactured by Scarecrow and spread through the city's water system. In one impoverished section of the city called the Narrows, the plan works: the toxin is released, and the Narrows falls into chaos.

"We can bring Gotham back," Batman tells Lieutenant Gordon. And while the reconquest of the Narrows isn't detailed in either *Batman Begins* or its sequels, you get the sense that bringing the region back to law and order would resemble what the comic book Batman deals with in 1999's *No Man's Land* series, where he and a few critical allies take back the city one block at a time.

Again, fitting. Fear isn't something that can be wiped away in an instant. Fighting that irrational terror is a matter of reclaiming control bit by bit until we are masters of ourselves again.

Another quick anecdote before we move on from Scarecrow—one related to the *No Man's Land* saga. The city of Gotham, ravaged by earthquake and disease, has been quarantined from the rest of the country. Most of its citizens have been evacuated. Stragglers—criminals, cops, and a few ordinary people—stayed behind, eking out a fitful existence in a truly lawless place. The Scarecrow naturally stayed behind too, a symbol of the terror that clutches at Gotham's remainders. He prowls through the city to find what havoc he can wreak and discovers a church filled with people, burning books against the winter cold.

"Barbarians!" Scarecrow thinks. "I have never known a cold so bitter that it must be staved off with books. Gotham is insane . . . and terrified! One can only wonder what keeps this condemned monstrosity from giving up altogether." Then Scarecrow discovers a book these cold, wretched survivors don't and won't burn: the *Holy Bible*. "Ahhh . . . of course," he says.

Scarecrow slithers into the company's midst and becomes one with them, slowly twisting their faith in directions it shouldn't go. First, he encourages the priest to compromise his values (Falcone would be proud) and hide a crate full of automatic weapons—more valuable than diamonds in the wasteland Gotham's become—for a warlord. Then he tells a rival gang about the stockpile, and the gang members promptly decide to claim the weapons for themselves. And so, out of fear, the folks living in the church grab the weapons and walk into the streets, ready to kill anyone who would take the guns from them. And the Scarecrow stands in the background, egging them on and waxing philosophic. "*When hell goes to war with itself,*" he tells us with a grin, "only the devil comes out a winner."

Scarecrow reminds Christians that the church is not immune to fear. In fact, this scene is a powerful metaphor of what we see happening all too often. We've always known that the world is a scary place; the tenets of our faith are pretty clear on that point. Christians, for most of our collective history, have walked by faith in the shadow of fear. In the United States, Christians have long held nominal sway over the culture. But in an age when religion runs weak and suspicion flows deep, we sometimes feel as though our faith and values are under attack. And how do we respond? Sometimes our fear makes us compromise: we embrace things we have no business embracing, perhaps hoping the culture around us will like us more—or if not that, simply let us be. Sometimes we turn against the world, twisting our open-handed faith into a closefisted sect, where we bellow back at the godless world that persecutes us. In our fear, legitimate or not, we shield ourselves in myriad ways, making it nearly impossible to do the hard work God has called us to.

Fear makes us a little crazy.

But the Scarecrow doesn't come out a winner. Despite all his efforts, the situation settles down and the congregation turns on him.

"I never would have imagined that their fear and hopelessness would drive them to this," he tells us. "It is a more hideous reaction than I ever dared dream. Now I am to become a martyr to my own solitary cause! How positively glorious!" But then Huntress, one of Batman's allies, "saves" Scarecrow, telling the people to consider, oddly, the virtue of Scarecrow's mechanisms.

"There's great power in our fear!" she says. "It can be used to fuel hatred and viciousness, yes—but it can also remind us how much we love those things we fear to be threatened. . . . Let us thank him for reminding us how much we still have to lose." And so instead of ripping Scarecrow apart, the congregants embrace him—rendering his fear impotent with the power of their forgiveness and love.

## RA'S AL GHUL: ZEALOTRY

As freaky as the guy is, Scarecrow doesn't qualify as Batman's primary adversary in *Batman Begins*. Dr. Crane and his powerful hallucinogen are merely tools in the hands of a more powerful adversary.

In Nolan's telling, Batman might never have come to be had it not been for Ra's al Ghul. The two are very much alike in both style and substance. Both have a penchant for theatricality. Both look impressive in black. And both crave justice like a dog craves sausage.

But they differ on what justice looks like. Batman wants to usher bad guys into prison. Al Ghul wants to usher them into eternity. In his eyes, due process is a joke and mercy a weakness to be expunged from the ideal human soul like a virus.

Little wonder al Ghul was attracted to Gotham like a pumped-up antibody. His antiseptic sense of justice makes him a perfect foil not for Batman, but for Falcone. If the mobster is Gotham's rot, al Ghul is its fire. Falcone relies on compromise; al Ghul abhors it. Falcone is corruption; al Ghul is incorruptible. Each is the extreme of the other, and both are bad to their beating cores.

"Like your father, you lack the courage to do all that is necessary," al Ghul tells Bruce. "If someone stands in the way of true justice, you simply walk up behind them and stab them in the heart."

Hey, there's nothing wrong with devoting yourself to true justice, obviously. Let's give al Ghul credit where it's due. Falcone is easy to recognize as a bad guy. Al Ghul can't stand the likes of Falcone or anything his ilk stand for. If we were going by the old adage "The enemy of my enemy is my friend," we'd have to consider al Ghul something of a friend . . . wouldn't we?

But al Ghul misunderstands the strange, frail nature of humanity. Corruption is a part of all our lives in this fallen world, and it's part of life itself—philosophically, spiritually, and even scientifically. The minute we're born, we begin to decay, our cells replacing themselves bit by bit until our marvelous ability to regenerate finally fails us. We're constantly in a cycle of decay and renewal. In a very real sense, you're not the same person you were last year or even last month. Corruption is a part of who we are.

Perhaps that's why the Christian doctrine of spiritual regeneration is so resonant. It feels as though it's about the only way to blend our innate propensity to corrupt and compromise with God's unfailing sense of justice. We fail; we're forgiven. We die in sin; we're born again. We shed our sins as we shed our skins, and we're recrafted in Christ's love, reaching ever closer to what we're truly meant to be.

Al Ghul isn't looking for rebirth, though. He's looking for perfection. He won't tolerate weakness. He is idealism without a crumb of compassion, justice without a pint of pity. And in fighting villainy, al Ghul becomes a villain himself.

He has lots of company.

Now, zealotry isn't all bad. Jesus counted Simon the Zealot among his disciples, and some pretty heroic individuals might fairly be classified as fighting zealously for their causes. And frankly, you'd hardly say that Batman lacks crime-fighting zeal. But zealotry untempered is inherently problematic.

The original Zealots—Jews who advocated rebellion against Rome in the first century AD—were history's first terrorists, according to some historians, attacking and killing Jew and Gentile alike to cleanse their homeland. And most zealots throughout history, be they the ruling class or a small sect of outliers, have shared a fondness for fear. The Spanish Inquisition used fear of torture and damnation to root out folks seen as infidels or heretics. Fascists of the twentieth century—zealots not for God but for an all-encompassing, fanatical political system—rose to power through fear, creating bogeymen from ethnic minorities and sowing terror among the opposition through thuggery.

So it shouldn't surprise us that al Ghul uses fear—Scarecrow's horrible hallucinogen—to bring Gotham to its knees. It has always worked before; why not now?

We know why, of course. Al Ghul runs into someone who knows his techniques. Batman had been afraid, but he has conquered his fear, and in so doing, he conquers Ra's al Ghul, too.

## TWO-FACE: DESPAIR

If Ra's al Ghul is a would-be hero who overshot goodness into insanity, *The Dark Knight*'s Two-Face is a hero who simply crashed and burned.

Harvey Dent, as we've seen, was Gotham's anointed champion: Lieutenant Gordon called him the city's white knight. Batman told him he was "the best of us." Dent asked the people of Gotham to believe in him, but in the end, he failed their trust and became a horrible parody of both Batman and his own better self.

Two-Face is Gotham's most tragic figure, his potential undermined by the disaster that took his love, destroyed his face, and scarred his soul. His faith—in goodness, in justice, in himself—was torn from him when Rachel died. Dent sees no design in his suffering, no purpose in his pain. He feels the weight of what he sees as a cold, careless universe. His new faith is no faith, and he aims to be the hopeless, heartless, godless god's ultimate prophet by killing or saving people through the flip of a coin.

"You thought we could be decent men in an indecent time," he tells Batman, holding Gordon's own son with the apparent purpose of killing him. "But you were wrong. The world is cruel, and the only morality in a cruel world is chance."

Dent's conversion to Two-Face isn't as far-fetched to us as it might first seem. Granted, we probably don't know too many people who have had half their faces neatly burned and then turned to a life of crime. But we know the damage despair can do to our faith.

It's not as if we weren't warned. "Here on earth you will have many trials and sorrows," Jesus tells us (John 16:33). Most of us have experienced pain, from the death of a loved one to an out-of-the-blue betrayal to the unexpected loss of a lifelong dream. It's not like we're expected to deal with these trials with a forced smile or stoic resolve. We grieve. We get angry. We wail and moan. We might not slap on sackcloth and pour ashes over our heads like they used to do . . . but we might consider it if we thought there was any chance it would take away the pain. Sometimes we ask God some pretty pointed questions or rail against the afflictions he seems to throw our way. And sometimes we may feel as if we've lost all hope. "Your fierce anger has overwhelmed me. Your terrors have paralyzed me," the psalmist tells his Lord. "You have taken away my companions and loved ones. Darkness is my closest friend" (Psalm 88:16, 18).

But for the faithful, hope returns . . . eventually. That's what having faith is all about, trusting and hoping in something greater than us, something higher. "Where there is still hope, there is no defeat," writes the theologian Dietrich Bonhoeffer. "There may be every kind of weakness, much clamor and complaining, much anxious shouting; nevertheless, because hope is present, the victory has already been won."

Despair is not just hope's absence in Bonhoeffer's eyes, but its rejection. Many Christians say they embrace Jesus' sacrifice on the cross but can't see their own suffering as anything but unmitigated evil. "How much grumbling and resisting, how much opposition to, and hatred of, our sufferings, has that revealed within us, and how much betrayal of our own principles, how much standing aside, how much fear, when Jesus' cross so much as begins to cast a tiny shadow on our own lives?" he says.

Two-Face betrayed his principles when his own suffering grew too great. This is not to minimize those sufferings. What Two-Face went through would have been enough to shake anyone to their core. How many of us would fall into despair in the force of such a gale? How many of us would cry to the heavens in anguish? Two-Face sounds very much like a despairing Job three millennia before: "He has stripped me of my honor and removed the crown from my head. He has demolished me on every side, and I am finished. He has uprooted my hope like a fallen tree" (Job 19:9-10). The real difference between them is that Job, in his anguish, was still talking with God—questioning him, shouting at him, accusing him. Two-Face, living in another time and another world, has nothing and no one to turn to.

"Why was it me who was the only one who lost everything?" Two-Face demands of Batman.

"It wasn't," Batman answers.

Batman lost Rachel too—the woman he loved. He lost Harvey Dent, Gotham's white knight, its hero without a mask, to a mad despair. And because of how the situation unfurled, both of these losses were at least in part Batman's fault. If anyone had reason to despair, it was Batman.

But he doesn't lose hope, doesn't lose faith—even in Dent himself. He tries to rescue Harvey from his despair until the very end, even allowing Two-Face to shoot him. Only when Two-Face is about to kill Gordon's little boy does Batman treat him as an enemy.

Despair is the archenemy of hope, and hope is at the core of what Batman is all about.

## CATWOMAN: AMORALITY

Batman has trouble hanging on to a girlfriend. While Superman and Lois Lane have been together longer than Laurel and Hardy, the Dark Knight seems to reboot his love life with each film. According to Wikia's DC Comics page (at dc.wikia.com), Bruce Wayne has had eighteen serious love interests, more or less—making him the Elizabeth Taylor of the superhero world.

But only one woman seems to have truly made a lasting impression on our man in black, one strong enough to bedazzle Batman for more than seventy years, from her 1940 introduction to 2012's *The Dark Knight Rises*: Selina Kyle, aka Catwoman.

It's curious that the two of them get along so well. Batman is a paragon of virtue and goodness. Catwoman typically treats virtue and goodness like so much kitty litter. That Batman and Catwoman don't try to kill each other (more often) is akin to Rush Limbaugh confessing a "thing" for Cher. I mean, opposites attract and all, but really?

Perhaps it's not completely outlandish. Batman's favorite feline fiend is one of superherodom's most ambiguous villains. If we examine the line between the good guys and the bad, we find that Catwoman often walks it like a tightrope. If she spends more time on the evil side of the ledger, it's not from any particular conviction. Rather, it's because she thinks it's a little more fun. She can do good things for bad reasons and bad things for the best of motives. Even her past is precocious: her backstory morphs every time she updates her outfit, and she has more getups than Lady Gaga during awards season.

Some narratives suggest Selina Kyle's alter ego is a product of trauma and abuse. In Tim Burton's 1992 *Batman Returns*, Michelle Pfeiffer's Catwoman comes about after her boss tried to kill her by pushing her out a window. Her secret identity is tied to the pain she's endured. And when Michael Keaton's flawed Batman sees her, he remembers his own pain and assumes that they are, essentially, warped reflections of each other.

"Don't you see?" he tells her. "We're the same—split right down the center."

But Batman learns in that film, and throughout history, that he and Catwoman are more like two sides of a coin than a mirror image: one heads, the other . . . ahem . . . tails. While they both share a fondness for alter egos and a propensity to go out at night, the motivating purpose behind the pair couldn't be more different. Batman uses his costumed persona to take a stand against the forces that created him. Catwoman stands for nothing. Traditional morality? Can't be bothered. Catwoman is all about the immediate, the sensate. If she wants something, be it a diamond necklace or a date with Bruce Wayne, rarely does she question whether she should, but whether she can and how quickly. She's the Cyndi Lauper of the superhero set: girls just want to have fun.

No wonder she tempts Batman. Her philosophy is enticing—and increasingly popular. Granted, society's not rushing out to the streets en masse to steal twenty-four-karat baubles, but more than a few folks express serious disdain for society's norms. They preach a life of "no limits," brag about how they're the type to break the rules, to break boundaries, to break the law, if necessary. "After all," they tell us, "what good is a free society if we can't be completely free? Why get married if we like to have sex? Why not lie if it gets us out of an uncomfortable conversation? Why not cheat?"

"An' it harm none do what ye will" is what modern Wiccans say, and while there aren't a whole lot of Wiccans spreading their own gospel, there's a great many people who could get behind their one-sentence summation of ideal morality.

Catwoman takes it a step further, of course. Her propensity to pilfer *does* hurt people . . . but they tend to be rich people or bad people or both, which makes her heisting hobby feel a bit more forgivable, to her and to us. And I think Batman, bound (as we shall see) by his own rigid code, may sometimes envy Catwoman and her sense of freedom, if not her ethos. She seems able to do something Batman hasn't quite mastered: she can have a little fun. In a time when Gotham seems to suffer under a perpetual haze of gloom, Catwoman can be vivacious and charming and crack wise with the best of 'em.

Despite all her obvious faults, maybe Batman sees in Catwoman one of God's most challenging directives: to live in the moment and enjoy life as it comes. We're supposed to enjoy the gifts God has given us, life most of all.

So it really is too bad that Catwoman, so busy relishing life, has completely forgotten its Author.

Catwoman is a live-and-let-live sort of woman, not inclined to take orders and not inclined to give them. She won't judge you for smoking weed or cheating on your boyfriend, so don't get on her case for stealing that necklace. Do you like Jesus? "Dandy," she'll say. Hare Krishna? "Whatever floats your boat." Her god is Catwoman, and she's rewarded in this world, not the next. If you asked about her thoughts on salvation, she'd likely tell you it's up to us to save ourselves—and any rewards to be had are taken, not given. So grab them while you can and let the moralists burn. A pox on rules, regulations, justice, and mercy. Live for today. Live for yourself.

In *A Million Miles in a Thousand Years*, Donald Miller writes, "[I] wonder if the reasons our lives seem so muddled is because we keep walking into scenes in which we, along with the people around us, have no clear idea what we want." Which brings us to an interesting counterpoint: if Batman is attracted to Catwoman because of her freedom, Catwoman must be drawn to the Dark Knight because of his stability—a stability coming from Batman's sense of purpose. And their relationship helps show us the best way to go.

Batman may be attracted, or even tempted, by Catwoman's carefree life. But he never seriously considers leaving his own calling. The same cannot be said of Catwoman: the attraction of purpose is too strong, and all the fleeting joys of flicking whips and robbing jewelry stores can't compete. And so we see that she sometimes teams up with Batman or falls into a relationship with him. Actually, in one of DC's alternate universes, she reforms permanently and marries him. But mostly she staggers between her two natures: she reforms, then backslides, reforms again, and backslides again. She longs for the stability Batman has found and wants it for herself, but she can't seem to escape the prison of her self-styled freedom.

Lots of us are a little like Catwoman, I think. We're drawn in by the lure of the world. We do things we ought not do, go places we ought not go. We drink or party or sleep around because, hey, it's fun (we tell ourselves). We feel free and alive and so comfortable in our own skin and we think for a moment that those skin-deep pleasures, those sensate moments, are what life's all about.

But then most of us (though not all) grow up. We get a

little older and maybe a little wiser, and we gradually come to a realization that we find a little shocking: what we thought was so much fun really wasn't. We just kind of thought it was for a while. What we mistook for freedom was actually the opposite. What we took to be the joy of life turned out to be simply a placeholder—a momentary blip in a life that was meant to be so much more.

I think Catwoman feels, at times, the same compulsion locked away in all of us: the desire to do what we were *made* to do. For Catwoman, that desire is in a wrestling match with her more superficial, sensate passions. And chances are, she'll never get full resolution. But if she did turn into a full-time good guy—if she did follow Batman's example and lived not for herself but for something else—I think she'd find that the division inside her would begin to heal, that maybe she wouldn't be split down the center anymore.

## BANE: ADDICTION

In *The Dark Knight Rises*, Catwoman shares the screen with another villain, lesser known but far more muscular. His comic book résumé has one achievement unmatched by any other Batman baddie—an accomplishment that proved to be out of reach for the Joker, the Penguin, and Ra's al Ghul. His name is Bane, and comic book aficionados know him as "the man who broke the Bat."

Crafted in 1993 by DC's Chuck Dixon, Doug Moench, and Graham Nolan, the pumped-up pounder was designed to be Batman's most formidable enemy—someone who harbored a singular desire to destroy the Dark Knight. He was born in the notorious Peña Dura prison on the island of Santa Prisca (named after a Christian martyr). He was supposed to live there for the rest of his life, literally punished for the sins of his father. He quickly proves that he belongs behind bars in his own right, killing for the first time at the tender age of eight. But he's not just a mass of misused muscle. Under the tutelage of a visiting Jesuit priest, he reads his way to real power in Peña Dura, becoming the smartest criminal in the joint.

Bane becomes too smart, too powerful for his own good. Prison officials had been experimenting with something called Venom—essentially steroids on steroids—for some time, but the stuff kept killing its subjects. Bane, they figure, might be the only man who can withstand the Venom, and they are all too right: Bane survives and escapes—both prison and the island.

What he isn't able to flee is the Venom itself. Hopelessly dependent on the stuff, he injects it directly into his brain every twelve hours through a series of implanted tubes. If he goes too long without it, he's gripped with unspeakable withdrawal symptoms—perhaps horrible enough to kill him.

Bane is an addict, a slave to the very thing that gives him power.

Of all the stumbling blocks we've seen so far, addiction is perhaps the most obvious and most insidious. On the surface, it seems like these unhealthy compulsions wouldn't, or shouldn't, be much of an issue for us. I mean, we know what makes addicts out of other people, right? We've been taught since grade school to stay away from drugs and cigarettes and have been warned for years about alcoholism. Health experts talk about food addictions, celebrities discuss their crippling sex habits, and pastors warn men about how terribly addicting pornography can be.

It seems, then, that if we know certain things can be unhealthy, we'll stay away from them, yes? It's not like we're locked in Peña Dura, having Venom pumped into our noggins without a say in the matter. Lots of the substances that can spark addiction can be easy to avoid if we put our minds to it. You gotta look long and hard for crack cocaine, for instance (in the neighborhoods I frequent, at least). And while porn is disturbingly easy to get these days, you still have to search for it most of the time. Issues with food are trickier, given our natural need to eat, but once we learn what sorts of food might trigger an unhealthy craving, we'll be able to just stay away from the candy machine and steer clear of the Häagen-Dazs, right?

Well, so it might seem . . . for people who have never dealt with addiction.

When pop/jazz singer Amy Winehouse died in the summer of 2011, it wasn't exactly a surprise. After firing off two brilliant albums, including 2007's Grammy-winning *Back to Black*, Winehouse quickly became far better known for her drug and alcohol abuse than her music. She'd make a go at rehab, but she'd never spend much more than a week getting help. Her fans watched her spiral down through disastrous concert appearances and tabloid rags.

She was losing it; everyone could see that. Winehouse's

story, we all suspected, wouldn't end well. Maybe she herself knew that. But she couldn't, or wouldn't, stop the fall. After she died, Maia Szalavitz—a former addict—wrote for *Time* about the true horror of addiction: "Contrary to popular belief . . . it's not the euphoria that hooks you. Instead, it's the ability simply to feel OK, the silencing of that voice of self-hate and the small sense of adequacy that comes in those quiet moments."

Every addict knows that once you hit a certain point, the stuff you're hooked on doesn't make you feel strong or giddy or powerful or sexually satisfied: it just makes you feel okay. And we're desperate to feel okay.

"There is a God-shaped vacuum in the heart of every man which cannot be filled by any created thing, but only by God, the Creator, made known through Jesus," French philosopher and mathematician Blaise Pascal once said. I believe that's true. Addicts, without the sense of God's love and grace and acceptance, try to wedge all sorts of things into that God-shaped hole. But it's not just *those* people—those non-Christian addicts—who feel the vacuum. Even when God is with us, we still can feel empty—a product, I believe, of our physical separation from him. So whether we know God or not, it's tempting to try almost anything to feel less empty. And for a while, things like porn or pot or a new purse from Macy's seem to do the trick.

Truth is, addictions are horrible and wonderful, beautiful and brutal. They provide a refuge or serve as a salve for this fragile, fallen world of ours when God can feel distant. For Bane, his Venom literally provides him an escape, a way to free himself from the horrible prison he grew up in, not that much different from how real-world addicts use substances to escape their own circumstances. Addictions give us the illusion of safety and control, even as we slip ever further away. Most important, our cravings by their very nature distract us from God and the business he has for us. What was found becomes lost, what was sighted grows blind.

In the DC story arc *Knightfall*, we see in Bane the illusion of power and security that our habits can give us—at least at first. But they can break us too, just as Bane broke the Bat.

Batman's no addict. His only compulsion in *Knightfall* is, as always, to save Gotham City. But his struggle still holds some parallels to the addictive experience, and they begin at the very outset.

"I escaped . . . for one reason only," Bane tells Batman. "To find you . . . and to break you." But Bane's no dummy. He knows the Dark Knight's a pretty formidable adversary. So before he faces Batman himself, he forces the superhero into a wicked trap. He lets loose scores of Batman's old adversaries from Arkham Asylum, forcing the superhero to fight them. From the beginning, Batman finds himself under Bane's inescapable influence. Batman retains the illusion of free choice, yet in truth, he has none, just as addicts find their own freedom to make choices taken away. Bane has set up the gauntlet, and Batman must run it.

As the saga wears on, Batman grows weaker, yet his quest to reach the end of the maze grows ever more compulsive. "Stop complaining," he tells himself, torn and bloodied.

"Keep moving. Your problems don't matter. You don't matter. Only *Gotham* matters."

On one hand, we can read this—rightly—as Batman sacrificing his safety and health for the city he's determined to protect. But it also echoes an addict's single-minded quest to feed a craving: you can lose your job, your family, and your health, all because of the single-minded pursuit of a fix. Indeed, *Knightfall* shows Batman pushing away those who would help him, those who plead for him to rest—halfhearted interventions to save the superhero's strength, perhaps life. But to no avail. Batman shrugs it all off.

And as he does so, Bane watches. "He is not ready to be broken," he says. "Not quite yet. When he is, I will know it. . . . And then the pieces will stay broken."

Bane will know it, just as our own addictions seem to sense our weaknesses. In the end, Batman—bloodied, bruised, nearly broken—faces Bane not on Gotham's mean streets but in Wayne Manor. Bane knows his adversary so well that he figures out his real identity (just as our addictions know us for who we are). So he shows up on Batman's doorstep to destroy him.

After a mighty fight, Bane lifts Batman over his knee and snaps his spine—another deeply symbolic move—leaving him literally broken. "Broken . . . and done," Bane says.

But Batman, true to form, is only physically shattered. It isn't easy, but eventually Bruce Wayne regains his health and puts on the cowl again. And the next time he faces Bane, he wins.

For the addict, Batman's recovery is an important moral. As crippling as addictions are, they *can* be overcome. Not easily, but with time, perseverance, and heroic effort, they can be subdued.

## JOKER: ANNIHILATION

And so we come to the end of Batman's gallery of rogues, where we face the most famous and diabolical of them all.

Batman's other villains carry threads of ourselves in them—our all-too-human propensity to despair or fear, our predilections for addiction or corruption. Even in the midst of their evil, most of Batman's enemies still have understandable, even relatable, goals: Carmine Falcone wants to take over Gotham City. Ra's al Ghul hopes to destroy it to create something "better." Bane wants to break Batman to prove *he's* better. Two-Face struggles to make sense of our cold and empty universe, while Catwoman sees herself at its center.

But the Joker in Christopher Nolan's *The Dark Knight* is something altogether different. While other evildoers look to impose order—their order—on the world, the Joker strives for chaos. They want to build; he wants to obliterate. They twist; he annihilates. He represents not the darker inclinations of our fallen selves but the fall itself—our impulse to destroy, to rebel, to fight against everything and everyone, to take what is and turn it to what was, to pull down whatever's pure and noble and true and leave it a smoking, shattered wreck. The Joker is filled with emptiness, lit with darkness. He speaks to infernal impulses to wipe away everything, even ourselves.

As Alfred Pennyworth tells Batman in *The Dark Knight*, "Some men just want to watch the world burn."

I don't know if there's ever been a more gripping depiction of pure evil in cinema than Heath Ledger's unforgettable Joker. And it's strangely fitting that Batman's most famous adversary would feel so much like Eden's silver-tongued snake or Faust's clever demon Mephistopheles. There's something of the truly infernal about him.

In the Bible, Satan tempts Eve in Eden, prods God to bring harm to Job, and tries to cut Jesus down to size in the wilderness. He's a fallen angel, we're taught: once the beautiful Lucifer, banished from heaven for rebelling against God, he now serves as heaven's accuser, its adversary, warring against the whole of creation.

When I was a child, I was always puzzled by Satan. Why, if the battle's already won, does he keep fighting? It didn't make any sense to me, and when I asked my Sunday school teacher about it, she was no help at all. She told me to hush up and not ask such questions.

Maybe through Nolan's Joker I partially understand: he lives to eliminate. He's beyond reconciliation, knowing he can never create, as God does. He can only destroy, and so, as much as it's in his power, he just wants to watch the world burn.

Unlike Lucifer, we really have no idea where the Joker comes from in *The Dark Knight*, why he is like he is or does what he does. He comes on a cloud of chaos, it would seem, a force of will more than man. It's very much like the original Joker in the Batman comics, before writers saw fit to endow him with his very own origin story (and then another and another). The Joker simply *is*—as disturbing an origin as we could ever imagine. But that doesn't keep him, in the movie, from crafting his own story. "Wanna know how I got these scars?" he asks repeatedly, seamlessly spinning lie after chilling lie—fitting for a character reflecting the Father of Lies. The truth means nothing to him; destruction is everything. And what is a lie but the destruction of truth?

In some ways he resembles Loki, Norse mythology's oft-malevolent trickster god, making mischief wherever he goes and playing jokes only he thinks are funny. Like Dante's demons from *Inferno*, he torments evildoers almost as much as the good guys. Like Faust's Mephistopheles (or the devil in Charlie Daniels Band's "The Devil Went Down to Georgia"), he's an expert deal broker, convincing the mob to practically sell its soul in exchange for Batman's head. He tries to get a ferry full of innocents to sell theirs as well, encouraging them to blow up a boatload of criminals to save themselves.

Nolan's Joker is, above all, a master tempter—a smooth, sick snake brandishing an eerie charisma that attracts as well as repels. In a strange, horrible way, he'd not look too out of place in Jesus' wilderness, asking the Son of God to compromise just a *little* to call upon a crowd of angels or change stones into bread.

He throws Harvey Dent into the terrible arms of nihilistic despair, turning him into Two-Face. "It wasn't hard," he tells Batman. "You see, madness, as you know, is like gravity. All it takes is a little push!"

When he needs to make a quick getaway from Gotham's holding cell, he convinces an officer to beat him. "Do you want to know why I use a knife?" he tells the detective. "Guns are too quick. You can't savor all the little emotions. You see, in their last moments, people show you who they really are, so in a way, I knew your friends better than you ever did. Would you like to know which of them were cowards?" The ruse allows the Joker to turn the tables on his attacker and escape.

Most important, though, he tries to corrupt Batman—and us along with him. Chaos, he tells us, is the only consistency in the universe. To build is an illusion. Destruction is the only reality.

"You see, their morals, their code, it's a bad joke, dropped at the first sign of trouble," he tells Batman. "They're only as good as the world allows them to be. I'll show you. When the chips are down, these . . . these civilized people, they'll eat each other."

"I'm not a monster," he says. "I'm just ahead of the curve."

As Christians, we might believe the Joker more than Batman does. We know how flawed the world is. We might have a better understanding of how frail we are too. We may long to be good, but we're so often bad. We know under whose jurisdiction our earthly realm lies right now. We know the Joker is in his element.

And yet there is reason for hope—not in ourselves, but in the one who made us.

"The earth was formless and empty," reads Genesis 1:2, "and darkness covered the deep waters." The Joker longs for a return to nothing and nothingness—a world torn asunder. Nothing begets nothing. Nothing is eternal.

Except with God.

"Let there be light!" God says, and there is light (Genesis 1:3). And in all his creation, God's light lingers. In the midst of our corruption and zealotry, our despair and fear, our selfishness and addictions, it stays, it glows, it grows.

We know there are two sides to the coin: one scarred and burned, the other reflecting God's perfect light. We know that each of us holds the coin in our souls. But those of us who are Christians know that we don't simply flip the thing to show the world who we are—or perhaps more fairly, who we want to be. It's not chance that determines which side we show; not fate, not circumstance, not even addiction or emotion. *We choose.* We choose who we're going to be each and every day, every hour and every minute. We choose what we'll show the world: our own sinful natures, or a perfect, pure light, not *of* ourselves, but reflected *in* ourselves, a light we can't take credit for but can embrace all the same.

Embracing this light is more than just a matter of rejecting the darkness. We need to do more than turn our backs on our fallen natures, the Scarecrows and Falcones and al Ghuls and Jokers that gallivant in our own frail natures. To reflect the light, we must first find it. And strangely, sometimes the best way to do that is to close our eyes.

## Chapter 4

# SUBMISSION

*You're gonna have to serve somebody.*
—Bob Dylan

**WE'VE GOTTEN A GLIMPSE** of the all-too-fallible darkness that lurks behind Batman's cowl. We've seen how human he is, doing his work without the superpowers that mark so many of his costumed cohorts. We've met the villains who haunt Gotham City and have found that many of them are just the flip side of Batman's (and our own) personality and character, virtues warped in a funhouse mirror, the darker side of a two-headed coin. Many of these bad guys think Batman isn't all that different from them—and they never get tired of telling him so.

"You *complete* me," the Joker tells Batman in *The Dark Knight*. "You *are* just like me," the serial killer Zsasz gloats in the comic series *Knightfall*. "But it's thrilling, isn't it? To be both hunter and hunted, knowing deep inside you *deserve* to be brought down." It's practically mandatory for the villain du jour to compare himself to his adversary.

So maybe it's not too surprising that every now and then the bad guys try to get Batman to join their fiendish fraternity, to turn to a life of evil. And even if they know that Batman's a lost cause and would never turn to the dark side, that doesn't stop them from trying to frame him so it looks like he has.

"To destroy Batman, we must first turn him into what he hates the most," Catwoman tells Penguin in *Batman Returns*. "Namely, us."

Those of us who have followed Batman a good long while know, of course, that our man in black can't be turned. But how do we know? Why, when we've seen how many traits he shares with his nefarious nemeses, would he not dip his toe into the gushing spring of crime?

It can't be because he's a hero. We've seen far too many good guys fall for us to assume they're exempt from changing their allegiances. Just look at Macbeth or Anakin Skywalker. Study up on King Saul or Judas Iscariot. It happens in professional wrestling all the time. And we've seen it happen often—far too often—in real life, from politics to the pitcher's mound to the pulpit. We've watched our heroes laid low by their own faults, our role models fall from grace. Name a sport, look at a profession, and we'll see plenty of disheartening examples of just how easy it is for the good guys to go bad. What makes Batman so different?

## "YOU'RE NOT THE BOSS OF ME!"

If you look at most of Batman's main evildoers, you'll see that for all their differences, they share a certain trait in common: they don't deal well with authority.

Which, when you think about it, makes sense. Criminals by definition have trouble following society's rules and regulations. If they followed a given set of laws, they'd be law-abiding citizens and not criminals at all. But when you get to the top of Gotham's heap of hellions, their loathsome aversion to taking orders from *anyone* takes on truly pathological proportions.

Sure, we see villains form alliances every now and then. Sometimes they form dastardly societies, complete with secret headquarters and membership cards and, presumably, the occasional convention in Reno. But any archnemesis worth his or her salt won't take orders from anyone for too long. Some, like Falcone, want to be the authority—to climb to the pinnacle of power in Gotham's shady underworld. Others want to destroy authority—either to replace it with something "better," as in Ra's al Ghul's case, or to watch the whole city burble its last, like the Joker. Still others—Catwoman comes to mind—just don't like being told what to do. Strip away their power, their mystique, and their never-ending supply of henchmen, and most villains sound suspiciously like preschoolers prone to bite. "You're not the boss of me!" they'll say to anyone who might suggest otherwise, and they'll blow up a warehouse or two to make their point.

I should pause here and note that it's not always a terrible thing to question authority. At least I hope not. I've been asking annoying, impertinent questions most of my life, and for a few years was able to make a living at it. If someone's going to tell me to do something, I want to know there's a good reason to do it. And if a good reason isn't forthcoming,

I tend to dig in my heels. There's a bit of that preschooler in all of us. And frankly, I'd like to think that's a good thing now and then.

"Unthinking respect for authority is the greatest enemy of truth," Albert Einstein once said, and we've been told through experience, through our culture, and sometimes by our authorities themselves to put it to the test now and then. "Don't trust anyone over thirty," baby boomers were told in the 1960s. Gen Xers were told to "think outside the box" or "color outside the lines"—gentler twists on the same authority-doubting theme. The United States itself was brought about as a challenge to authority, and the country's most hallowed documents were crafted in such a way as to limit institutional power and preserve the freedom of us common folk.

It shouldn't be too surprising, then, that some of America's most popular champions are those who sometimes flout the law. Wyatt Earp and Doc Holliday are probably the best-known heroes to come out of the wild, Wild West—even though their O.K. Corral showdown with the Clantons should have, strictly speaking, gotten both of them thrown in the clink pending an appointment with the hangman. Jack Bauer, from Fox's long-running show *24*, was so zealous in his defense of America that he broke most of its laws on a daily basis. We love our pirates, our musketeers, our vigilantes—folks who do the wrong things for the right reasons or the right things on the wrong side of the rules. Antiheroes are as American as baseball, apple pie, and *Jersey Shore*.

Batman is one of our most enduring antiheroes. These days he operates well outside Gotham's legal code, and the authorities aren't always so sure what to make of the guy. Would anyone dare arrest him for assault? Pull him over for speeding? I doubt it. Nobody can compel him to obey Gotham's metropolitan ordinances or traffic codes. If there is anyone who would be prone to shout, "You're not the boss of me!" it'd be our cowled crusader. He kneels before no one, bows to nothing.

Or does he?

To find an answer, we must again look back to Bruce Wayne's graduation ceremony with the League of Shadows in those cold Nepalese mountains.

We've already been introduced to the event: a farmer-turned-murderer is brought before Bruce. "Crime cannot be tolerated," Ducard says. "Criminals thrive on the indulgence of society's understanding." And he puts a sword in Bruce's hands.

It's clear what Bruce is being asked to do. It's a demand from a man who has been Bruce's most effective teacher, the closest thing he's had to a father for a long time. Moreover, it's what the society in which he lives—the League of Shadows—*requires* him to do. In a society where the sanctity of law is so zealously upheld, this is its most important: to punish those who break it with swift, certain severity.

We've seen how Bruce answered. We've seen how that answer gave birth to Batman. "I'm no executioner," he says, apparently rejecting the only authority he knows.

But let's look closer. In rejecting one master, he acknowledges another—one far greater than the man sitting enthroned in front of him or the man standing beside him. He submits to an ideal—an understanding that there are some truths that surpass human whim and will and even rule: an unseen king, if you will. Yes, he tells al Ghul, "You're not the boss of me," in no uncertain terms, and winds up burning down al Ghul's temple for good measure. But in that moment, he acknowledges another's mastery over him.

## AN UNSPOKEN AUTHORITY

I must reiterate here that Batman is not an explicitly *Christian* hero. We don't know if he has said the sinner's prayer or watched *Fireproof* or attends church regularly (though he'd likely make a kick-butt middle school youth leader). He's a pretty private guy and not all that chatty. Considering that Batman runs around with a cowl over his face, I guess we can't expect him to prattle on about his concept of God.

So when I say that Bruce Wayne submits to another "boss," I don't want to suggest that that "boss" is our Lord and Savior. He was not "born again" there in the League's temple in any traditional Christian sense. But what happened in that moment isn't that dissimilar to what we feel when we find faith and make it our own.

"One must pass through the flame in order to know death and embrace it," writes Henry Miller in *The Time of the Assassins: A Study in Rimbaud*. "The strength of the rebel, who is the Evil One, lies in his inflexibility, but true strength lies in submission which permits one to dedicate his life, through devotion, to something beyond himself."

"True strength lies in submission."

But what is Bruce Wayne submitting to?

Assume for a moment that Bruce Wayne lives in a godless world, a place as cold and merciless as Two-Face believes it to be—a world where we flawed and constantly failing humans are the ultimate arbiters of what is right and wrong. In such a world, the very words *right* and *wrong* have little meaning. They are subjective, flighty things, a "bad joke" in the eyes of the Joker. In such a world, the Joker is indeed "ahead of the curve." Catwoman is perhaps pursuing the only possible means of happiness such a world allows. Idealists such as Ra's al Ghul might strive to bring pattern to this chaos, plastering over the inevitable doom we all face with a thin facade of order.

And what of our hero? In such a world, what reason does he have to put down the sword and let this criminal live? The only explicit moral authority in that place—the League of Shadows—deems the execution just. Moreover, its leader orders Bruce to carry it out. If morality is determined by man, then by the authority of the most moral men Bruce knows, this criminal deserves to die. Even setting aside the League's marble-hard ethics, there is no reason to spare him. Pragmatically, Bruce stands to gain power, prestige, and authority if he sees this bloody ceremony to its natural end. To refuse means facing the same end as the criminal in the cage. Even if he shakes off the League's sense of morality and embraces the moral-free void, it still makes sense to kill the man. Looking at this scene through the moral lens of a Falcone, a Scarecrow, a Joker . . . to mete out the ultimate punishment makes perfect, pragmatic sense.

"For your own sake," Ducard tells him, "there is no turning back."

And without a sense of what lies beyond mortal morality, there would seem to be no choice.

And yet, this is what we hear:

"I'm no executioner."

He submits, but not to the League's misguided morality, nor to the chaos that engulfs so many of his future rivals. He submits to a higher authority, an acknowledgment that there is a right and a wrong in this world, there is good and evil, justice and mercy. And when he rejects the executioner's sword, he risks his life for that authority. In three words, he tells the League, the world, and himself that there are things that transcend Darwinian understanding—ideals worth living and dying for. There is something within us that surpasses bone and blood and the binary code of the brain; there is something outside us, perhaps, that cares how we live. He acknowledges the human soul and spirit and thus bends his knee before the force that guides it. Our Dark Knight pays fealty to a King he may not fully know.

## ON BENDED KNEE

The Christian faith is explicitly pinned to the concept of submission. "Follow me," Jesus tells his disciples, and they do—leaving behind their homes and jobs to serve this man from Nazareth. "Follow me," he tells us as well.

In the Christian community, we've gotten so used to the lingo surrounding the Christian walk—that we're "the hands and feet of God," that we have "new life in Jesus," that we're "his followers"—that we lose sight of how alarmingly radical Jesus' directive is. We're not "following" Jesus to the grocery store or subscribing to his Twitter feed. We're following Jesus' example in everything we say and do, becoming his stewards on earth. Just as he gave his life for us, we're supposed to give ours to him. "Since we have died to sin," the apostle Paul writes, "how can we continue to live in it? Or have you forgotten that when we were joined with Christ Jesus in baptism, we joined him in his death? For we died and were buried with Christ by baptism. And just as Christ was raised from the dead by the glorious power of the Father, now we also may live new lives" (Romans 6:2-4).

If we're Christians, we're not the boss anymore.

It's a scary thing, submission. Terrifying, really. When we truly swear fealty to God—when we promise him that our lives are his to do with as he wishes—there's a frightening possibility that he might take us up on that offer. Just ask Paul. I'm sure that if he had his druthers, he would have settled down as an unassuming tentmaker after becoming a Christian. Or maybe those would just be *my* druthers. I'm not one to make a ruckus, and I have a serious issue with discomfort. But the apostle doesn't hesitate. Instead, he gallivants across the known world, preaching this new, radical faith to the masses. And if the masses decide to stone him, no matter: Paul just bandages his wounds and goes right back.

And he was just on the vanguard of centuries of Christians who found their lives turned upside down after being called to Christ. When I was a religion reporter, I had an opportunity to interview people who dumped nice, secure livelihoods for a radical manifestation of faith. I've lost count of the number of Christians who told me something like, "The last thing I wanted to do was quit my job and start a soup kitchen," or, "I had no intention of giving up those seats on the fifty-yard line so I could teach Sunday school." But they'd say they had an overwhelming sense that God wanted them to do it. I don't know *how* they knew . . . and sometimes neither did they. "I just knew," they'd say.

"Only he who believes is obedient," writes Dietrich Bonhoeffer in *The Cost of Discipleship*. "Only he who is obedient believes." It's a telling statement, implying that faith and action go hand in hand. To become a Christian means being open to accepting strange, sometimes unthought-of directives for reasons that aren't always entirely clear. To become a Christian means accepting that life could take a drastic, even ludicrous, turn—much as it did for Bruce Wayne.

Consider the radical changes Bruce makes in his own life after his critical showdown with the League of Shadows. One minute he's a virtual vagabond, deliberately eschewing his upbringing and home to live a dangerous, hand-to-mouth existence in the wilds of Asia. The next he's on a plane back to Gotham, harboring the absolutely laughable ambition to become the city's unpaid protector. Think upping your weekly offering ten bucks or bringing a friend to youth group is a show of commitment? Bruce decides to spend the family fortune on capes and crime labs and to fritter away his free time fighting crazy criminals. Now *that's* an out-of-the-box calling. What sort of person makes a life change like that without radical submission? Without that submission, without an understanding that there is something greater out there, the principles of the comic villain look far more reasonable.

All those who call themselves Christian have declared their fealty—and thus submission—to God, whether they fully understand it or not. For many Christians that commitment often culminates in baptism. It's a sort of induction ceremony, where we symbolically swear our allegiance to our God and Savior. And while I believe that baptism is more a ceremonial marker than a literal line of demarcation between sin and salvation (the real moment of redemption takes place very often in isolation, during a halting, heartfelt prayer), it still marks a critical moment in our lives. And in some ways it's not all that different from Bruce's own baptism by fire. Before we accept Jesus into our lives, we're in the wilderness, scratching out a living the only way we know how. Afterward, our lives are radically redirected: we've reclaimed our birthright, and we're on our way home.

From that moment on, we're "saved." Nothing can separate us from God's love. We're on our way to heaven. Our sins are forgiven. We're in the club, and no one can revoke our membership.

But while all that's true, submitting to Christ isn't a one-time thing—say a prayer, get dunked, and that's the end of it. For some of us, we must remember to submit every day, every hour . . . sometimes every minute. Otherwise it's too easy to forget that our lives are not our own.

## IT'S 11 P.M.; DO YOU KNOW WHERE YOUR SOUL IS?

Batman doesn't punch a time clock. He has no employer to impress, no paycheck to collect for being Gotham's leading crime fighter. His work is done on a strictly volunteer basis. And even then, the comparison isn't quite right. Volunteers are still expected to show up at certain times and perform certain duties. There's no one to tell Batman what to do and no one explicitly asking him to do it.

It'd be easy for the guy to take a night off. Or a week. Or a month. Even if he was missed, so few people know his true identity that it's hard to imagine that anyone would show up at Wayne Manor and scold Bruce for his dereliction of duties. And even if they *did* know how to find him, who would really blame him? It'd be asking a lot of someone to risk his life night after night with no promise of reward or even thanks. Sometimes Gotham's boys in blue would rather give our Dark Knight a pass to jail than a hearty handshake for a job well done.

There's only one person who pushes Bruce Wayne into Batman's cape and cowl: Batman himself.

It's pretty remarkable when you think about it. Consider the costs involved in this curious hobby. The financial outlay required alone is enough to make Donald Trump tremble. Batman has geeked-out cars, motorcycles, boats, and planes. He has a cave equipped with the latest crime-fighting gadgets, and getting Internet service down to the Batcave must have cost a pretty penny. Batman's body armor isn't something Alfred can just pick up at the local Army surplus store, either.

The cowls themselves have to be special ordered, and we learn in *Batman Begins* that those orders have to be enormous to avoid suspicion—like, ten thousand units enormous.

"Well, at least we'll have spares," Bruce tells Alfred.

We know Bruce is rich, so maybe he can afford to write massive checks for another gross of batarangs. But no matter how wealthy Mr. Wayne may be, he can't buy more time, and fighting crime takes a lot of it. Bruce spends his days as a wealthy playboy and his nights as a costumed crusader. He's got to take time to train, too, to keep his body and mind in tip-top condition. It's hard to imagine the guy getting much sleep most nights, but he must get a little, or else he'd be too groggy to do his job. We must assume that Bruce hasn't spent a lazy night at the mansion watching a movie or playing a video game for ages. Indeed, Bruce Wayne has made some staggering sacrifices to keep Batman alive and effective on the streets of Gotham night after night. And yet sometimes he sacrifices even more.

Remember, our Dark Knight has no special abilities, no superpowers to heal quickly or to survive on little snippets of sleep. When he gets stabbed, shot, beaten, or bitten, he bleeds and bruises just like you or I would. Thank goodness Alfred is not only a talented valet but a well-dressed paramedic as well.

"Know your limits, Master Wayne," Alfred warns Bruce in *The Dark Knight* as he patches him up again.

"Batman has no limits," Bruce says.

"Well, you do, sir."

"Well, I can't afford to know 'em."

There are very few things that would compel a sane man to tackle the evil lurking in Gotham's mean streets at the rise of every moon. Radical, unflappable submission to a cause is the most rational and reasonable among them. Batman didn't just submit to his ideals, to his calling, in the mountains of Nepal. Every day he renews his commitment, and every night he submits again—even at the risk of discovery, injury, and death.

Many Christians all over the world know something about that sort of commitment. Here in America, if the mall up the road won't play "Silent Night" come Christmastime, some Christians feel as if they're being persecuted. But to my knowledge, the mall cops aren't yet rounding up shoppers carrying Bible apps on their phones. There are countries where Christianity is a crime, places where your faith could get you killed. In environs like that, it becomes an act of submission and faith not only to become a Christian but to stay a Christian. Every day people wake up and pray to their God or hold a Bible study knowing that this simple act could get them in lots of trouble.

But it's not just Christians who live under the threat of severe persecution who must recommit—or should I say resubmit—to their faith with each rising or setting sun. "If any of you wants to be my follower, you must turn from your selfish ways, take up your cross daily, and follow me," Jesus tells us (Luke 9:23). My pastor says that the sound of our alarm clocks beeping in the morning is God's call to work. Even those of us who live in relatively safe, relatively wealthy places can benefit from reminding ourselves frequently—daily—that we're not the boss of ourselves. As Paul writes, "God saved you by his grace when you believed. . . . Salvation is not a reward for the good things we have done, so none of us can boast about it. For we are God's masterpiece. He has created us anew in Christ Jesus, so we can do the good things he planned for us long ago" (Ephesians 2:8-10).

I was officially baptized in a tiny Baptist church when I was seven years old. I made the decision during one of our church's interminably long altar calls, and not (from what I remember) with the best of motives. I had always been curious about what the baptismal looked like, and I figured the only way I'd ever see the inside of it was by getting myself dunked.

I'm sure there was something else going on—I arrived at the altar crying pretty hard—and my seven-year-old self was pretty committed to becoming a Christian when I had the obligatory talk with the minister. But I never mentioned my ulterior motive to him, and because of that I spent a good chunk of my childhood wondering whether my baptism "took."

See, seven-year-olds can take things quite literally, and I figured there was something magical about the ceremony itself, that the submersion in my church's "holy" tap water (they filled the baptismal with a garden hose) would protect me from the fiery awfulness of hell. And I think it's possible that in my old-school Baptist church, they may have believed that the moment of baptism *was* of prime importance for God. I know many Christians believed it then, and I know many believe it today: if you don't get your hair wet for Jesus, he won't keep it from burning in the ever after.

But as I got older, I wondered whether my semi-insincerity might have damaged my prospects of having a real relationship with God. It made me wonder whether I was really "saved," and if I wasn't, if that's why I still felt the temptation to lie or whatnot. And naturally, once I hit puberty and a whole bunch of temptations and sins showed up in my psyche, I *really* started to worry.

Now, obviously, this was terrible theology. Had I talked with my parents or pastors and gotten some more clarity on the subject, it might have saved me a lot of existential stress. But it led me to take up a curious and not altogether bad habit: I'd recommit my life to Christ every six months or so. I'd ask God to forgive me for the myriad things I'd done wrong lately and pray for salvation all over again. Surely this is bad doctrine in itself and wholly unnecessary. But it kept me mindful that Christianity, like healthy weight loss, is a lifestyle, not a fad.

I think that evangelical Christians can sometimes take their salvation for granted. Many of them, like me, were baptized (and far more sincerely) at an early age. Probably their definition of salvation was more clearly defined for them than it was for me. But because of that, I think we can forget that becoming a Christian is more than a moment in time: it's a lifelong journey. And as such, we're always walking into a greater understanding, and hopefully appreciation, of what being a Christian is all about. I've been taught, and I believe, that once you commit your life to Christ, you can't ever be kicked out of the club. But I also believe there's more to being a Christian than just that one moment of submission.

It's a bit of a paradox, really—like the paradox of being a parent.

When my son, Colin, was conceived, I became a father. If I had left for good the minute after I learned the results of the pregnancy test, I'd still be a father. No matter how far I'd run or how hard I'd try to forget, it's a fact that would be obvious to anyone with a genetic scanner. And yet to be a *good* father means to get up every day and tell myself that that's what I'm going to be. I change diapers and attend tea parties and build LEGO towns and play catch and save for college and talk and scold and praise and worry and love. And it gets to the point where being a father isn't something I do; it's who I am.

The same could be said of Bruce Wayne and Batman. No one would say that Batman is a sham that Bruce throws on every now and then when the mood strikes him. No one would dare suggest that he dons the cape and cowl for, say, a couple of hours a weekend when he's feeling particularly motivated to pay homage to his ideals.

Batman isn't something Bruce Wayne does; Batman is who Bruce Wayne *is*. That doesn't mean he always feels like being Batman. Most likely, considering the challenges and threats he faces night in and night out, there are times when he wonders whether it's worth it, whether he should hang up the utility belt and enjoy his wealth for a change, spending it on a private island instead of ten thousand armored cowls.

But he doesn't. He has submitted to a higher authority, a

greater ideal. He bends his knee and bows his head to something greater than himself.

Sure, it's a tough life. It's expensive and dangerous, and it never leaves Bruce enough time for a proper vacation. But that's okay, because Batman isn't something he does. It's who he is. In submitting his own will to a higher calling, he finds himself. It's what he was built for, in a way.

And by extension, so are we. We're at our best when we're setting aside our own desires and serving others. When we *forget* ourselves, we *become* ourselves—our true selves, the people God designed us to be.

We've submitted to God, and if we've taken that submission seriously, we're to be about God's work. Batman knows what it means to submit and what it costs. That's why it's wholly appropriate that when Batman's called to work, it's often through a beacon we know as the bat signal—a light that shines on high.

## Chapter 5

# CODE

*I have had my day.*
*The dirty nurse, Experience, in her kind*
*Hath fouled me—an I wallowed, then I washed—*
*I have had my day and my philosophies—*
*And thank the Lord I am King Arthur's fool.*
—Lord Alfred Tennyson, Idylls of the King

**IN FRANK MILLER** and David Mazzucchelli's *Batman: Year One*, a young, inexperienced Batman surprises a trio of petty thieves standing on the fire escape of a high-rise apartment building.

"The costume works," he thinks as he eyes their shocked faces from above. "Better than I'd hoped." Wearing cape and mask for the first time, he torpedoes downward and lands in the midst of the crooks, who are gaping, afraid, and still holding their pilfered TV sets and record players. One of them, more scared than the rest, backs away . . . and tumbles over the rail.

They're twenty stories up.

"No!" Batman cries in his mind. "I'm no killer."

He shoots out a hand and grabs the boy by his heel, holding him, screaming, above the street below. "Can't be older than fifteen," Batman thinks. "A child—just a child." Teeth clenched, Batman holds the boy even as the burglar's two friends hit and kick him. One picks up a television and brings it down on the back of Batman's head, the electrical cord snaking in the air like a whip. Still Batman holds on, blindly firing a kick behind him to fend off an attacker while still clinging to the kid's sneaker-clad foot. He senses another blow coming at him from the right. He snags the leg of his new assailant and twists, bringing the guy down hard on the landing's metal floor. Finally free of attackers, Batman hauls up the third boy—now unconscious, maybe from fear—and sits panting among his KO'd prey.

"Good thing he blacked out," Batman thinks. "If he'd kept thrashing . . ."

He leaves the thought unfinished, dangling in the city air.

The fight on the fire escape wasn't quite the operatic melee that Batman's later battles would be. He wasn't taking on the Joker or Two-Face or even the head of a crime syndicate: just three petty thieves with their arms full of electronics. But at this early stage of Batman's career, it's still significant. It shows a code taking shape, a set of rules that Batman will adhere to come fire, flood, or a TV set to the back of the head.

Some might find it curious that Batman has rules at all. At first glance, the guy seems exempt from them. Even in those camp-filled days of the 1960s when Batman and Robin were fully deputized agents of the law, Batman's given free rein to do what he needs to do—from assaulting suspects to breaking speed limits with his rocket-powered Batmobile. In the grittier Batman stories, like *Year One* or the Christopher Nolan films, the Dark Knight is a vigilante—a black-clad paradox who breaks those who break the law. In those narratives, the only reason Batman's not in jail is the police can't catch him.

And yet in spite of all Batman's wanton lawbreaking, the guy's practically synonymous with law—so much so that he can come across as very nearly prudish. In the 1960s television show, that was the gag: he loved law and was so enamored of order that he'd cut short a pursuit to teach a handful of children about the dangers of jaywalking. *That* Batman was the sort of square who'd be almost insufferable in real life, the nerd in school who'd always remind the teacher about the homework assignment, or the guy in church you'd never, ever confide in for fear he might judge you. Even in more recent times, when Batman and Gotham's law enforcement share an uneasy truce, the main point of friction seems to be not that Batman doesn't take crime seriously; it's that no one else—not even fellow superheroes—takes crime seriously enough for Batman's taste.

Batman's got respect for rules, no doubt about it. Boy howdy, does he respect them. They're just sometimes a different set than we're asked to follow. And while they're not mutually exclusive, they are sometimes . . . different.

"He has identified the white and the black, or the right and the wrong, and lived by that code much more strictly than anyone else does," says Dan DiDio, senior vice president and executive editor for DC, in the documentary *Batman Unmasked: The Psychology of the Dark Knight*. "Laws are open to interpretation. Batman's law is not."

I'm not going to argue that Batman's setting a great example for the rest of us to follow here. If you beat someone for, say, littering, I'm not going to show up at court in your defense. But we're going to give Batman, a fictional hero, a little bit of rope here and again and use him as an illustration of a simple truth most of us already know: that law and justice aren't always the same thing; that there are higher forms of truth than those we can discern through rules and regs and lawyers and judges.

When Batman acknowledged that good and evil aren't just constructs of society or products of law—when he came to see that he was beholden to a moral ethos that transcends human understanding—he must have known then that man's laws were not fully adequate to address it. And so he found himself well on his way to discovering a new law: a code more rigid than any on the books, more reflective of a nearly divine sense of both justice and mercy. There's nothing particularly new about this code of his. The basic tenets are those inculcated by other organizations, other groups whose members believe that they, too, are instruments of good—servants to a just, merciful Master imperfectly understood.

They don't call Batman a knight for nothing.

## A KNIGHT IN SHINING BODY ARMOR

We're all familiar with the medieval knight—or, at least, we think we are. In real-world Europe, knights were mostly landed gentry fostered by the age's feudal economy. They paid fealty to a king (or sometimes a more powerful noble), and if the king needed assistance in winning a border skirmish or putting down a peasant revolt or fighting an out-and-out war, he'd call on these knights to come help. Naturally, they'd come, armed to their eyebrows with broadswords and axes and splendid chain mail suits. Some of the most famous knightly orders, like the Knights Templar and Hospitaller, were specifically created to follow a very Batman-like mission: to protect innocent travelers from those who meant them harm.

But as nifty as these guys looked thundering through their battlefields, the knights of story and song were even cooler. While real knights were apt to be as petty, cruel, stupid, or silly looking as the next guy, those who populated the age's poems, fables, and fairy tales were almost sure to be handsome and brave and ever so virtuous. The paladins in the stories of Charlemagne or the knights who sat around King Arthur's round table were the superheroes of the age—stronger, smarter, braver, and better than the average Middle Age gadabout.

Yeah, we know all this. To this day, we sometimes still talk about real-world heroes—a brave politician or conscientious citizen or even a baseball player who hits a ninth-inning home run—in terms of these heroic knights of yore. They "ride white horses," "charge into battle," "slay our dragons"—all phrases that conjure images of warriors covered in armor, sword and shield in hand, bravely facing any foe. And the main reason most of us know today what knights were all about is that they—both the fictional and the factual—adhered to a code of chivalry, a broad litany of rules and virtues that any knight worth his salt was bound by.

Now, granted, there never was an official code drawn up by the pope and inculcated into the whole of Europe by decree. The tenets of chivalry differed from region to region and changed from generation to generation. Moreover, the knights of our imaginations were always able to adhere to these flexible chivalrous standards far better than the real ones could ever hope to. But that doesn't mean knights weren't expected to behave a certain way, and those expectations were often drawn out in literature and enforced by the knights themselves.

The knights from *The Song of Roland*, composed around the turn of the twelfth century, boasted a whole host of chivalrous virtues: They were expected to be brave, honest, and courteous, always ready to right a wrong, protect the innocent, and respect a woman's honor. They fought relentlessly, prayed constantly, and eschewed (at least in theory) any sort of monetary gain from their exploits. King Arthur's warriors were popular for both their valor and piety, earning a form of immortality by searching for the Holy Grail. These knights were, in some ways, role models—the first real folk heroes Britons could call their own. These were not the pagan heroes of ancient Greece and Rome, but Christian heroes, made mighty through prayer. Roland, Lancelot, and Gawain supplanted Achilles and Hercules, and the concept of a "knight in shining armor" was born—long before knights even wore shiny armor.

From nearly the beginning of Batman's career, the Caped Crusader was meant to exhibit more than a passing resemblance to these medieval forebears. Like the typical knight, Bruce Wayne was born into a wealthy, landed family, complete with a castle-like manor and a coat of arms. (And even if the Wayne family overlooked an official knightly monogram, the black-and-white bat symbol would look mighty fine on a shield.) As Batman, he carries weapons, wears a kind of armor, and, while he doesn't have a heavy warhorse at his disposal, he's got scads of horsepower in the Batmobile, which is at least as cool. Just like his knightly predecessors, he bought all of his battle accoutrements himself. Even Batman's relationship with Robin bears a resemblance to that of a knight and his squire.

Note that Batman's unofficial early biographer drew the line between "ye knights of olde" and Batman and Robin in a 1943 story ("The Batman's Biographer," in *Batman* No. 17).

"Gee, they're brave just like the knights of King Arthur's time, aren't they?" one child gasps, listening with rapt fascination to the biographer's stories.

But nothing links the Dark Knight closer to his chivalrous ancestors more than his code—one not that different from ideals espoused by Roland or Arthur or any of literature's sprawling order of knights. While he might not rigorously follow the speed limit or avoid jaywalking, you can always count on Batman to adhere to a handful of self-steeled directives.

## TO FIGHT FOR FAITH

Knights were a pious lot. In literature, King Arthur's cadre of fighters earned their greatest fame searching for the Holy Grail while Charlemagne's paladins were embroiled in a life-or-death struggle with Islamic infidels. Historically, scads of knights hailing from a host of disparate countries embarked on Crusades to the Holy Land, hoping to remake Palestine into a Christian country (and they even succeeded for a while). Knights didn't just swear an oath of obedience to a king; they swore it to God. And there were even orders of knights who bypassed national fealty altogether and instead offered allegiance directly to heaven.

Batman, as we've seen, is not a direct descendant of the knight in terms of his abject piety. But the Caped Crusader does believe in something higher than himself, and he pays allegiance to that belief without reservation.

"He's clearly a man with a mission, but it's not one of vengeance," Frank Miller, who wrote both *Year One* and *The Dark Knight Returns*, told the magazine *Amazing Heroes*. "Bruce is not after personal revenge. . . . He's much bigger than that; he's much more noble than that. He wants the world to be a better place."

But it's more than that, too. It's not just a matter of want but also a matter of must. The world *should* be a better place, *should* be closer to an ideal that he and all of us have buried deep within ourselves.

The knights of old, in their chivalric code, promised to keep their faith, defend the church, and further God's Kingdom. They considered themselves, in a very real sense, spiritual warriors, casting their eyes toward heaven while trying to pull a bit of it down to earth.

Batman also yearns for a more perfect world (though perhaps he'd not dare call it heaven). "We will, we can, bring

Gotham back," he says to Jim Gordon in *Batman Begins*. He has a vision of a shining city on a hill—a place of justice and goodness, where children don't lose their parents in dark alleys and where superheroes can go back to being billionaire playboys. He knows that Gotham can be better, maybe even good. But it isn't there yet. And so, while keeping the vision of a better, safer Gotham alive in his own soul, he fights, night by night and block by block, to bring the city closer to that ideal.

Incidentally, Batman's insistence that there's something better out there is inherently judgmental. His belief that he can be instrumental in making Gotham better is, perhaps to some who don't share his vision or "belief," rather arrogant. Who are we to say what is good or bad? Who are we to force our values on others? Whenever we talk about making something *better*, we automatically assert an assumption that there is a better to be built—that values like good and bad, right and wrong, are more than subjective constructs: they're objective goals to which mankind can and should aspire.

Like it or not, Christians belong to that same camp. We believe in right and wrong. We believe that neither we nor our environs are all they could be—that it's important to improve ourselves and the world around us.

Critics of Christianity accuse us of being too judgmental, and they're often right. We can be petty and mean-spirited and silly, and we can cause people who might be interested in our faith to drop everything and run the other way.

But at the same time, I don't think we can turn our backs on a paradox in God's character that lies at the heart of our faith: while God forgives us our shortcomings—and I'm so thankful he does—he also cares about who we are, how we act, and how we treat those around us. He loves us and treasures us for who we are, but he also longs for us to reach higher, to become who he truly built us to be. He embraces our actual but pushes us toward our potential. He knows firsthand the *better* in all of us because he made us. And because of that, we're deeply aware of how much better our cities, our schools, and ourselves can be.

Batman is in his own flawed way keeping the faith. And that faith lies at the core of the rest of his code.

## TO PURSUE JUSTICE

Back in the Middle Ages, Europe didn't have anything like what you'd call a modern police force or judicial system. I'm sure most of the leaders of the day tried to do their best, but the idea of due process was a bit hazy. Law enforcement was at best inconsistent (heaven help you if you were accused of witchcraft and had an unfortunate wart on your nose) and at worst nonexistent. Most people couldn't count on much help if they ran into difficulty, and as a result, knights would sometimes serve—at least in literature and perhaps in real life too—as instruments of justice. Was a maiden's honor besmirched? A village harried by a nearby dragon? A gadabout throwing medieval litter into the king's moat? A wandering knight might be enlisted to find, capture, try, and even punish any impertinent evildoers at fault, sometimes within the course of an afternoon. It was assumed that knights (almost always pious fellows sanctioned by God himself in the stories) had a good handle on justice and could be trusted to take care of business. And most often they did.

But what if they didn't? What if the challenge was just too great? Or what if the knight simply wanted to call it a day, head home, and watch the eleventh-century version of *The Amazing Race*? What then?

That just wouldn't happen. Any knight worth his metal-buffing agent would never quit a gig. *The Song of Roland* insists that true knights must be paragons of perseverance. They can't just drop their shields and head for the hills at the first sign of a dragon. They can't let a little flesh wound get them down. And while perhaps not all knights—either real or literary—would be quite as tenacious as the limbless Black Knight in *Monty Python and the Holy Grail*, they were expected to fight the good fight until they literally could fight no more.

It's probably pretty obvious that pursuing justice is what Batman's all about. He's rarely one to hang back when it comes to fighting bad guys—not unless he's under the influence of some nefarious hypnotist's charm or ray gun. The whole reason Batman came to be in the first place was to clear Gotham City's streets of evildoers. And boy, does Gotham need the guy. The city can seem to be as lawless as Europe in the Dark Ages, what with all the crime and corruption at play. But if Gotham's thieves are indeed thick and its finest aren't all that fine, Batman fills the breach, making the town feel a little safer. He doesn't clean up moats or fight dragons, but he does tidy the streets and fight Penguins on occasion.

He has a deep intolerance of evil, and he'll do whatever he can to exorcise Gotham's temporal demons. In Gotham, Batman is about the only force its citizens can count on. And he pursues his purpose with furious tenacity. Sometimes, in fact, he can go a little overboard.

In *Knightfall*, the superhero pushes himself to the point of annihilation, fighting sickness, injury, and a who's who of supervillains, bringing them to justice one by one. He faces nearly a dozen (and an angry panther, too) as he claws his way nearer and nearer to the story's ultimate evildoer, Bane. Batman realizes that by the time he faces the final miscreant, he'll likely have nothing left to fight with. But he pushes on just the same.

"Isolate the pain," Batman groans. "Lock it away. Put it in a tiny box in a corner of my mind. I'm the city's only hope. I'm all that stands between these monsters and Gotham."

We have to admire Bats for his drive and be quite grateful that, even as we follow his example and strive to make things better around us, we still have the leeway to get some decent shut-eye when we need to. Most of us don't have a bevy of insane supercriminals to corral before dinnertime.

The tenacious pursuit of justice looks a little different in our world. It might lack some of the drama we see in Batman's, but that doesn't mean we're not enmeshed in the same sorts of struggles. Standing up for what we know is right—particularly when it involves standing up to those who are wrong—can be hard and discouraging and even frightening. I wish I could say I've always been Batman-like in this respect, but I don't want to lie.

One night when I was about eleven, my parents invited some friends over to dinner who also had kids—a girl of about six, around my sister's age, and a boy who was maybe fifteen. The boy also had a friend over, and all of us kids were sequestered in an adjacent room; we could see the adults if we peered through the open door and down the hallway, but we weren't really within conversational earshot, not unless everyone in one room got really quiet to hear what was going on in the other. But maybe that's exactly what the grown-ups should have done.

The fifteen-year-old boy and his friend spent the entire dinner making fun of the younger kids—how we talked or looked or ate. I was a particularly vulnerable target, with my glasses and buckteeth and unruly hair. I was skinny and pale and completely inept, a fifth-grade elephant man, I thought of myself. From painful experience I knew how vulnerable I was to being picked on. And I figured the only hope I had of surviving the dinner without crying was to be as silent and small as possible, hoping the two older boys would forget about me.

The strategy worked . . . after a fashion. "Look at that kid's teeth," one of the fifteen-year-olds would say amid a flurry of swearing. "He looks like Bugs Bunny." And then across the table my six-year-old sister would rise to my defense. "If you can't say something nice," she hollered, "don't say anything at all!" And the boys would swiftly train their acidic verbiage on her, mimicking her, swearing at her, calling her names that even in my public school upbringing I had never heard.

We couldn't tattle. It was unthinkable. So what did I do? I sat there, eating my food, praying dinner would be over and we could all leave and pretend the night never happened. I sat there, trying to protect my own shredded self-esteem as these teens tore into my little sister and her friend like hyenas on an antelope. I sat there. I *knew* I should do something . . . and I *sat* there. My sister, all of six, knew more about courage, more about Batman, than I did.

I wish I could get a do-over dinner. I wish I could stand up to those guys now. It wouldn't have mattered, of course . . . I was too weak to make a difference. But at least, maybe, I could have shown those guys that what they were doing wasn't right. I could have shown my sister that she deserved to be treated better, that we all did. At least I would have stood up for her.

"Not all monsters are bad, but the ones who are good never do what they could," the band Jars of Clay tells us in "Good Monsters." In some ways, maybe that's what separates the heroes from the monsters—in Gotham and at dinner tables. So often we hear stories about how a woman was hit by a car or a man was beaten nearly to death on a street corner and how people would just walk by, drive by, move on their way, and pretend they didn't see. Some people can't be bothered. Most of us read stories like that and are understandably appalled. We tell ourselves that we'd never be like that, that we'd stand up to the bad guys and try to make things better.

I'd like to think so. Hopefully I'm better now. But I wonder how often I have a chance to make something right and instead I sit still, like the "good monster" I am.

The pursuit of justice is about more than pursuing the unjust: it's about the just, too, protecting them as best we can.

## TO PROTECT THE INNOCENT

The knights in *The Song of Roland* were expected to safeguard the weak, care for widows and orphans, and fight for the benefit of all. These directives are inherently rooted in faith. Left to our own Darwinian impulses or sinful selves, it would be far more pragmatic to pillage the weak than care for them. Unless they're weak and rich, or weak and well connected (in which case they wouldn't be weak at all), it's unlikely we'd receive anything for our trouble. Care for widows and orphans? There's no profit in that.

But the literary knights of yore weren't interested in making a buck, and neither is Batman. When he was a child, he watched helplessly as his innocent parents died in front of him. Bruce Wayne could have been shot dead that night too. It would've been easy for the killer to pull the trigger one more time. He understands better than most of us what it's like to stand before the world, left to its mercy. And he knows what it's like to be an orphan.

Maybe because of this, or because of his fealty to his moral order (or both), he'll do everything in his power to save the innocent—even at the risk of his own life.

It's a trait we see in every movie, every book, and every television show ever made about Batman, and sometimes his zeal for safeguarding the innocent is so off the charts that it becomes comical.

In 1966's campy *Batman: The Movie*, our Caped Crusader discovers a bomb—one of those black, ball-like explosives you might see Wile E. Coyote use—in a saloon. He picks it up in both hands and runs out of the building, trying to find a safe place to dispose of it. But everywhere he turns, unlikely innocents block his way. He can't toss it over here because of a pair of nuns. He can't get rid of it over there because of a woman with a baby stroller. Behind him? Impossible: the path's blocked by a tiny Salvation Army band. Batman even tries to throw the thing in the water, but he's stymied in that, too: he sees a family of ducks out for an afternoon swim.

"Some days you just can't get rid of a bomb!" he laments.

But Batman's high regard for life is no laughing matter, for him or for us. Henri Ducard warned Bruce Wayne that his compassion was a weakness, and sometimes it seems to be. Many a villain has made a quick getaway as Batman tends to the injured or protects the innocent. In *Knightfall*, Bane incorporates Batman's compassion into his plans for the hero's downfall. But it's also what makes him a true hero. Without this critical bit of chivalry, Batman wouldn't be a hero at all.

It's here—caring for the poor, the hungry, the sick, the innocent—that most of us non-superhero types can make the biggest impact on our world. Frankly, we can make a bigger impact than even Batman could. While it's great to toss the occasional bulbous, black bomb into the drink, we don't run across those every day. The bombs we see aren't as obvious and are far less dramatic, but they're just as dangerous. We need not walk too far before we come face-to-face with poverty, hunger, and sickness, tragedies that haunt a staggering number of people in every city and every town in America, much less the world.

Churches and charities try to help these folks as best they

can, but the need is great. Most of these organizations are always looking for help: volunteers to dish out food, build playgrounds, or visit the elderly; benefactors who can give some much-needed and always-appreciated cash. Countless people want our help: abandoned children, drug addicts, families bound by poverty. They need it. You could even say they deserve it.

But could we help those who pushed them into their predicaments? Would we save the pimps, the drug dealers, the swindlers if they were in some serious trouble too?

Batman does.

And it's his curious penchant for saving the bad guys—the same fellows who are trying to kill him—that makes Batman particularly, albeit maddeningly, heroic.

## TO PROTECT THE GUILTY, TOO

Champions of old had no qualms about hacking down villains if they seemed to deserve it. Those swords of theirs were pointy for a reason. Knights were trained to kill, and rarely did they withhold a mortal blow if they thought it warranted. In literature, they were policeman, judge, jury, and if need be, executioner. And we are okay with that, for the most part. We're pretty forgiving of our heroes if they kill someone who has it coming. *Lethal Weapon*? The Dirty Harry movies? There's a reason those films made scads of money.

You'd think Batman would be the poster boy for sweet, cold revenge. Scarred by the murder of his parents, he dresses in all black to scare the boxers off Gotham's underworld. He's beholden to no man, unfettered by social propriety. Murderers and rapists wonder whether he's a man at all. Perhaps he's a ghost or a vengeful demon or a vampire out for blood.

And yet Batman doesn't kill—not if he can help it. It is, as he tells the Joker, his "one rule."

Not every narrative has strictly adhered to this one rule. In Batman's first couple of years in the comics, he'd rarely shed a tear if a baddie got his, and Batman would sometimes gun the guy down himself. Michael Keaton wasn't always merciful in Tim Burton's *Batman* or *Batman Returns*. In *Batman Begins*, the Dark Knight doesn't work too hard to save Ra's al Ghul from a fiery end. "I won't kill you, but I don't have to save you," Batman tells him.

But those are exceptions to Batman's rule, which has been on the books since 1940. It was then that the folks at DC said Batman would never off another villain, no matter how villainous he might be. And so Batman will often go to some serious lengths to save the lives of even the worst evildoers.

When the costumed pyromaniac Firefly sets the old Majestic Theater ablaze in *Knightfall*, Batman leaps through the flames and grabs hold of him just as Firefly, equipped with a set of glider wings, begins to float away.

"No!" Firefly shouts. "You'll kill us! Burn us alive!" And sure enough, the two plummet to the flames below.

"He deserves it," Batman thinks, the flames licking his costume. "Maybe we both do . . . but got to let him go . . ."

He does just that, and Batman falls as Firefly catches a thermal updraft. "Yes! You fool!" Firefly taunts as he soars to safety. "Sacrificing yourself—to save your own killer!"

Batman has no intention of sacrificing himself. Not yet, at any rate. Though already engulfed in flames, Batman shoots a quick, thin lifeline around Firefly's ankles and is carried past the fire's greedy fingers before Firefly manages to cut the rope. Batman smashes into, ironically, a fire escape ladder. He's alive. And more important to him, so is Firefly.

It's clear that Batman's no pacifist, but he understands the difference between justice and vengeance. And even as he sometimes *bends* the law, he understands that he cannot *be* the law.

In a sense, Batman takes a more Christian tack when it comes to justice than those pious and zealous knights did. Roland and Lancelot considered themselves to be Christ's instruments of justice and were thus somehow supernaturally imbued with the authority to not just save lives but take them as well. Batman knows better. He knows true justice is not for him to bestow. He'll do the legwork and let others pass judgment—even knowing that their judgments will rarely be perfect.

We can learn from Batman here, I think. He shows us that justice and mercy are not diametrically opposed ideals but values that work in unison. It's not exactly a "hate the sin, love the sinner" type of dichotomy, but in Batman's rough-and-tumble Gotham, that he hates the sin and doesn't *kill* the sinner is something we can sink our teeth into. And if we were all blessed with incredible strength and nifty utility belts and effective immunity from prosecution, I wonder how many of us would hold ourselves to the standards Batman holds himself to—particularly if we've suffered as deeply as he has.

Consider Batman's ongoing struggle with the Joker, the man who has inflicted more pain on the Dark Knight than perhaps anyone besides the thief who killed his parents. (And if you take Tim Burton's *Batman* account at its word, Joker was responsible for that, too.) The Harlequin of Hate, as he's sometimes called, has killed countless people over the years—including Jason Todd, a boy who once served as Batman's sidekick, Robin. Were we in Batman's black boots, would we be so quick to turn away from meting out ultimate justice? To not take matters in our own hands even when we knew it would ensure that the Joker never hurt anyone again?

In *Knightfall*, Batman—sick and wounded and run to the point of exhaustion—confronts the Joker yet again, this time in the company of Scarecrow, in a subway tunnel deep underneath the waters that surround Gotham City. The villains have in tow a terrified politician, Mayor Krol, bait with which they hope to hook a run-down, weary Batman and destroy him once and for all. Batman knows it's a trap, but it doesn't matter, because Batman has a code to follow: He must pursue justice. He must protect the innocent. Trap or no trap, he must do what he can.

First blood goes to the villains. Scarecrow sprays the hero with some of his fearful toxin—stuff that pulls your worst memories and fears from your psyche and forces them to haunt you—and Batman flashes back to Jason Todd's murder: the pain, the impotency he felt, the deeply felt cruelty of the Joker. He wasn't there when Jason was killed. But with the help of Scarecrow's poison, he sees it all.

The toxin doesn't have the intended effect, though. Rather

than being rendered harmless by it, Batman works himself into a rage to fight off its effects. And with images of Jason's brutal end still running through his mind, Batman turns his attention to the Joker.

"Jason Todd," he hisses at the mass murderer, the Joker's white face a mask of fright. "Jason Todd!" Batman hollers, kicking the killer. Batman beats the Joker silly, decades of anger and rage and who knows what else pouring into every blow, shouting Jason's name at every strike. He is, in this moment, a fearsome weapon—a veritable angel of death.

And yet we know that as Batman's fury reaches a terrifying crescendo, he's not at his strongest here, but his weakest.

And then, KROOM!" Scarecrow blows a hole in the roof of the subway tunnel, and water from the river above seeps through the wound.

"L-looks like it won't hold for l-long, Bats," the battered Joker says. "So you'd better m-make your choice—stop us . . . or save your 'phone-phreak mayor!"

But it's not a choice—not for Batman. Not with his code. "No way I let him kill another," he thinks to himself. "I've got to save Krol."

In the midst of all that pain, anger, and exhaustion, Batman is still a knight in the best sense: He will pursue justice. He will punish the guilty. But he will not risk an innocent life, nor take a guilty one. "I am no killer," he tells us, and time and time again he proves his words true.

He is a knight in the best of meanings, a knight in body armor riding a high-octane horse. This Caped Crusader is not perfect, but he stands by his code, as just and as merciful and as chivalrous as any that came before, adhering to its tenets with unwavering conviction.

Batman stands for something, and many of those values he stands for were first modeled in another hero, in a much different way, two thousand years ago. Unwavering justice. Unreasoning mercy. Righteous anger. Tenacity. Grace. Faith.

Batman's code is predicated on faith—not necessarily faith in the Christian God, but faith that there are such things as goodness and justice and that these things are worth fighting for, worth dying for. The world is fallen, he sees, and so is he. But at its core and at his own, there's something worth saving, something worth protecting. There is something worth redeeming.

# Chapter 6

# TOOLS

*Hence it comes about that all armed Prophets have been victorious, and all unarmed Prophets have been destroyed.*
—Niccolo Machiavelli, *The Prince*

**EVERY KNIGHT NEEDS** some armor in the closet, and the Dark Knight is no different. In *Batman Begins*, Bruce Wayne goes on a shopping spree of sorts for his dangerous pastime. He raids the research and development department of his family business in the quest for a suitable outfit. He finds one in a pricey prototype for infantry body armor.

"Tear resistant?" he asks Wayne Enterprises employee Lucius Fox as he examines the prototype.

"This sucker will stop a knife," Lucius says.

"Bulletproof?"

"Anything but a straight shot," says Lucius. "So what's your interest in it, Mr. Wayne?"

"I want to borrow it," Bruce says, "for . . . spelunking."

"Spelunking?"

"Yeah, you know, cave diving."

Lucius arches an eyebrow. "You expecting to run into much gunfire in these caves?"

Lucius isn't told of Bruce's plans just yet, but we know. Piece by piece, this rich man-about-town is building the Batman.

Batman is, in some ways, a miracle of technology. From his earliest days, he used crime-fighting gear that made traditional lawmen salivate, stuff so advanced that even his 1940s arsenal, with its hovering Batplane and Batgyro, might have modern-day engineers scrambling to duplicate them. From the suit to the Batmobile to the high-tech lab in the Batcave, the Dark Knight has the best equipment money can buy. It just makes sense, considering his lack of superpowers. In his quest to be an instrument for justice, Bruce Wayne needs some clever instruments of his own. He can't expect to rid Gotham City of bad guys while wearing a comfortable pair of sweats and driving a Honda Fit.

In Ephesians, Paul talks about the importance of strapping on some spiritual armor against spiritual enemies. "For we are not fighting against flesh-and-blood enemies, but against evil rulers and authorities of the unseen world, against mighty powers in this dark world, and against evil spirits in the heavenly places," he writes (Ephesians 6:12).

We've already seen that while Batman's adversaries are very much flesh and blood—they shed enough of the latter for us to know—they're also spiritual enemies of a sort: Catwoman can represent the pull of amorality, Two-Face the temptation to despair, Ra's al Ghul our inclination toward unforgiving zealotry. So while Batman's armor and utility belt are designed for use in the material world, I don't think it's too much of a stretch to suggest they might have spiritual components too—or at the very least, that they might help us talk about the more spiritual battles in which Christians engage from time to time.

Paul is pretty specific about the spiritual armor we're to strap on:

> Stand your ground, putting on the belt of truth and the body armor of God's righteousness. For shoes, put on the peace that comes from the Good News so that you will be fully prepared. In addition to all of these, hold up the shield of faith to stop the fiery arrows of the devil. Put on salvation as your helmet, and take the sword of the Spirit, which is the word of God.
>
> EPHESIANS 6:14-17

It makes me happy that Paul started his litany of armor with a belt, because that allows us to examine sooner one of my favorite pieces of Batman's arsenal.

## UTILITY BELT OF TRUTH

When I was a kid, I cobbled together my own Batman utility belt from various bits of household flotsam. The belt I was using already had a nifty compass for a buckle, so I didn't need to worry about that. (Not that Batman ever had a compass that I remember, but with Gotham's streets as crazy as they surely are, perhaps he should have!) I rolled bits of yellow construction paper into cylinders and stuffed in all the crime-fighting equipment I could get my hands on. I tied a plastic shower hook to the end of a roll of dental floss and used it as a grappling hook. I stole one of my mom's hairnets to snare the bad guys. And while I didn't have any gas pellets to fill my cylinders (they would've slid out the open bottom end anyway), my imagination certainly filled in the gaps.

But as cool as my utility belt was, it was a pale comparison to the real thing. Since the very beginning, Batman has been filling his belt with all manner of great gizmos: penlights and blowtorches, first aid kits and underwater breathing apparatuses, sliver-thin ropes and super-sharp batarangs. Batman's utility belt would make even the best-prepared Swiss army officer look at his pocketknife and shed bitter tears of gadget envy. The utility belt is at the core of Batman's power—an awesome array of offensive and defensive tools that can overpower foes and extricate the Dark Knight from almost any tight spot. Practically everything Batman might need during a night about town is somehow stored or connected to this belt in some way. Batman without his utility belt? Why, that's like Aaron Rodgers without his football helmet or Paris Hilton without a purse dog. And who knows? Perhaps in the old days, when Batman was more prone to wear tight-fitting spandex than the body armor we're familiar with in the later movies, maybe the belt helped hold up his briefs, too.

If we're Christians, we're all girded with truth—the

ultimate truth of who God is, who Jesus is, and what this life of ours (using broad strokes, mind you) means. That truth in itself is a powerful thing, one that allows us to see the world as it is but not lose sight of the divine seed in it all. It's true the world is a mess. It's true that we are too. We also believe it to be true that all is not lost—that we are still loved, still redeemable, and still have a chance at forgiveness and salvation.

It's on this truth that we attach the rest of our lives. It's on this truth that we hang everything else we're to be about. Once we know who God is, we know far better who we are and how we should be spending our time. The clarity of that truth brings a clarity to our own lives. It helps us see (like Batman's penlight), it helps us heal (like Batman's first aid kit), it helps us climb to new heights and swim through the murkiest of depths.

And sometimes being secure in our truth can help us keep our metaphorical shorts from falling down around our ankles. Nothing is quite so embarrassing as strutting around like all is normal but not having a shred of truth to keep our trousers hitched up. We've all seen people caught in embarrassing lies. Perhaps we've had it happen to us. I know I have, and I learned a long time ago that as embarrassing as the truth sometimes is (and trust me, it can be horribly embarrassing), it's not nearly so awkward as a fib laid bare. Maybe Richard Nixon would have served out his second term had he not lied. Maybe Bill Clinton wouldn't have been impeached had he come clean about his relationship with Monica Lewinsky. People, I've found, are remarkably forgiving of foolishness.

But when we lie, we're treating those we lie to as fools. And that's a harder sin to wash clean.

## THE KEVLAR BODY ARMOR OF RIGHTEOUSNESS

Back in biblical times, no one wore full suits of shiny armor. My guess is that hinged joints might have been a problem for ancient metallurgists, and even if they could manufacture them, they might have been a bit of a hindrance on the battlefield. After all, they really only came in vogue among the rich who could afford horses to carry them into battle and squires who could help lift them off the ground if they fell over. Fully armed knights charging into battle on foot, as the ancient Israelites were in the habit of doing, might have been slow and looked silly had they worn full suits of armor.

So with all those hindrances in play, it makes perfect sense that the ancient armorer would have focused on protecting the body's most vital regions: the chest and the head. And it was the breastplate that did the admirable job of guarding all of the soldier's most valuable innards.

The folks who make Batman's body armor don't have the sorts of limitations faced by the armories of BC-meets-AD Rome. Forget the dowdy bronze breastplates of Caesar Augustus's day: Batman sports trendy, bullet-stopping Kevlar. In the movies, naturally, our hero goes all out, wearing head-to-toe body armor. But in the comics, where Batman still seems to favor spandex as the core of his evening wear, the triple-weave Kevlar is positioned strategically around the Dark Knight's signature yellow-and-black logo, positioned right in the middle of his chest. That conspicuous bat symbol, Batman tells us, is an intentional target for gun-wielding bad guys: better they fire a slug or two into Batman's well-armored torso than at his less-protected face.

Most of us don't dodge gunfire on a night-to-night basis, but there are those who might want to do us harm. They might pepper us with rumors or pound us with innuendo or stab us with, heaven forbid, the truth of our all-too-often duplicitous lives and try to take us down through charges of hypocrisy or immorality. Hey, we've all seen what happens when people we respect and admire are caught in acts inconsistent with their stated values. Christians certainly aren't the only folks who can be caught acting duplicitously, but sometimes I think we're particularly vulnerable. It's amazing, really, how many of us can be quite, if you will excuse the expression, two-faced—how we'll condemn one sin while somehow excusing ourselves to commit another or even falling victim to the very same sin. There are folks out there who will blast infidels yet surf Internet porn sites; those who say they abhor dishonesty but cheat on their tax returns; those who tell their children to never fib and then lie to their faces.

How do we guard against such attacks? By being righteous, of course. If we live in accordance with our values, we won't be caught lying, cheating, or philandering because there's nothing to catch us doing. A blameless life is pretty good protection against the slings and arrows of a cynical world, and my guess is that Christianity would be better thought of today had Christian role models—be they pounding a pulpit on television or working at the corner church—more often practiced what they preached.

Wearing that metaphorical armor of righteousness is a pretty good way of guarding ourselves against false charges, too. Lies and innuendos will most likely bounce off it like Nerf balls. It's amazing, when you think about it, how simple it is. "That's all I have to do to keep the world from skewering me as a hypocrite?" someone might ask with a scratch of the head. "Live a righteous life? There's gotta be a catch." And actually, there is one. It's hard to wear this armor day after day. It's heavy and sometimes uncomfortable. I know lots of good people who have fallen into sins or habits they could have and should have avoided. Sometimes the armor fell at just the wrong time, and they were cut to the quick. Sometimes they corrected it on their own. And there have been times when I've let my guard down, and my righteousness has fallen to the floor with a loud and guilty clang. Maybe we *all* let our breastplates slip or fall at times . . . but I'd like to think there are those who really have mastered its weight and wear it as God intended. Undoubtedly, it does grow lighter with time. But I don't know if the weight ever completely dissolves.

It's hard to stay righteous, but Batman has understood the importance of doing so from the very beginning. In 1940's *Detective Comics* No. 38, the issue in which the Caped Crusader first meets Dick Grayson—the boy who would be Robin for the next several decades—he makes the lad raise his hand, Boy Scout style, and swear that they'll "fight together against crime and corruption and never to swerve from the path of righteousness." It's an important oath to take; we know that if our hero became unrighteous, he'd cease being a hero at all.

## THE STEEL-TOED BOOTS OF READINESS

Of all the accoutrements in Batman's wardrobe, his boots are perhaps the most boring. They don't come with wings or electrical charges. They don't have invisibility cloaks or hidden jet packs. According to Scott Beatty's book *Batman: The Ultimate Guide to the Dark Knight*, the hero's "steel-toed leather boots are augmented with Nomex-reinforced thermally-stable rubberized soles. Split asym slingshot heels flex with his ankles for full range of motion during building ascents." Sure, this isn't the sort of stuff you'd find in your off-the-rack pair of Converses, but it doesn't sound all that revolutionary, does it?

Maybe not. But what this description tells me is that with these things on, Batman's ready for almost anything. The rubberized soles give plenty of traction, and should an electrical current course through a damp floor, Batman will still be just fine. The steel toes protect his feet from any stray anvils the Joker might decide to drop and make for a nice bit of extra oomph should Batman decide to kick him in the chin. The boots aren't just nicely suited for scaling buildings, but for running and jumping and creeping in the dead of night.

And Batman has added one extra to the boot heel: a bat beacon, able to send off an ultrasonic signal that attracts flying rodents from all corners of Gotham.

"What is that?" a young Jim Gordon asks Batman, shortly after the hero pushes his heel button and the two begin to hear high-pitched squeaks coming toward them.

"Backup," the Dark Knight answers. Bats pour into the room, and Batman makes a dramatic exit.

We live in a world just as chaotic as Batman's Gotham—a place where we might be called on to walk or climb or run like crazy. These days, we can never be flat-footed; the era demands we be flexible, durable, and ready for anything.

I play a little tennis, but I don't play particularly well. And a big reason why I struggle is that I've never had good footwork. The feet, it seems, are key in almost any athletic endeavor. In football, accurate throws aren't so much a matter of arm strength but of foot placement. In baseball, you hear hitters talk just as much about their stance as their bat speed or concentration. When you watch professional tennis players on television, you'll notice that as they get set to return a serve, they bounce and run in place and hop from foot to foot with more alacrity than a puppy who's been lapping up Mountain Dew. You might say that lowly feet are the very (ahem) sole of athletic success.

Paul never knew or cared about the best techniques for returning a serve, but he did understand the importance of footwork. He knew that the biggest biceps or the brawniest core or the brainiest brain wouldn't be worth much in battle if the soldier was not sufficiently nimble—ready, as it were, for anything. And where does that readiness come from? From the gospel, of course—from being rooted in God's Word. He's not just talking about a passing familiarity with the Bible but an intimate embrace of it. It's that embrace—that understanding (as much as anyone can hope to understand such a rich and provocative work)—that allows us as Christians to be nimble. To be quick. To be ready for anything. When we know the spirit of the Scriptures so well that we don't have to think about them anymore—when we incorporate the truth of the Word in our everyday thinking as easily and seamlessly as a quarterback does his footwork—that's when we're ready for anything. And with that sense of readiness comes a sense of peace, a sense that whatever life serves us, we'll be in position to handle it.

But to be ready doesn't mean to resign ourselves to being on our own. This gospel of ours originates from our Maker and gives us our only concrete insight into his character and the character of his Son. Like Batman's sonic heel, it's tethered to a reality we can scarcely comprehend . . . and yet it tells us that our unfathomable Creator cares about us and listens to us. In short, the Bible tells us that God answers prayers. Sure, our own "boots of readiness" may be strictly earthbound, but that doesn't mean we can't look, at times, for some backup from above.

## THE CAPE OF FAITH

Capes, for all their inherent panache, are not a must-have superhero accessory these days. In the Disney/Pixar film *The Incredibles*, superhero fashion maven Edna deems them a dangerous impediment for costumed crime fighters.

"Stratogale! April 23rd, '57! Cape caught in a jet turbine! . . . Metaman, express elevator! Dynaguy, snagged on takeoff!

Splashdown, sucked into a vortex!" It's indeed a gruesome look at how impractical wearing a cape in the line of super-duty can be.

But Edna has never taken a long, hard look at Batman's scalloped cloak. While it might have been just a nice bit of flowing fabric back in his earlier days, the cape has become one of Batman's most compelling, complex, and versatile tools. Paul's shield of faith can "stop the fiery arrows of the devil" (Ephesians 6:16), and Batman's cape can do something like that too. In the comic book arc *Knightfall* and the forgettable film *Batman Forever*, it's shown to be fire retardant, protecting Batman from flaming catastrophe. It's said by some to have a thin layer of Kevlar woven into its fabric, too, shielding its wearer a bit from gunfire.

It can also serve as a literal cloaking device. When Batman hides behind its billowy mass, it can be hard for the bad guys to pick out just exactly where the hero might be standing or where to aim. And just like the shields of old, Batman's cape can be used offensively, too. Its edges are weighted, so it can pack a formidable thwack when Batman whirls around. Imagine getting snapped with a towel—with a roll of quarters embedded in the business end. That's what I imagine it might feel like to get hit with Batman's cape.

But the cape has one other ability worth mentioning—one never approached by any shield I know of. In *Batman Begins*, the hero uses his cloak as a hang glider, allowing him to soar through the city like an oversized paper airplane.

For us non-superheroes, faith can do much the same things in our lives. If righteousness can guard against some of the world's more obvious frontal attacks—assaults upon our character and morality—our faith can shield us from what we might call flank maneuvers. Being righteous is small consolation when we're oppressed by stress or heartache or sickness, the day-to-day stuff that saps our strength and distracts us from the job and joy of life. The fact that we're not swerving from the path of righteousness doesn't help us much materially, psychologically, or spiritually if we're in desperate need of a job, if we're caring for a sick child, or if we're failing algebra. Sometimes it can even be an impediment. It's so tempting to start asking God why we're suffering, why he allows us to hurt when we've done everything he's asked us to do. If Satan or fate or God himself sets before us trials and tribulations, anguish and pain, righteousness alone can't protect us from that pain.

But faith, in its own way, can.

Faith isn't a magic force field. It doesn't encase us in a diamond globe, safeguarding us from all unpleasantness. We're gonna feel pain in this world, Jesus tells us, and most of us have been around long enough to know that he's right. But faith can act a little like Batman's cape.

When Batman's careening through Gotham's latest catastrophic fireball, wrapping himself in his cape for protection, I'm sure he feels the heat. I'm sure he sweats. But the cape keeps him from burning up. When he uses the thing to ward off, say, a hail of arrows, I'm sure he can feel each one of the arrowheads bounce off the cloak—and one or two shafts might even punch a hole in the fabric. But the cape keeps them from shish kebabing his back.

Our faith doesn't keep us from suffering. It doesn't save

us from the anguish of losing a parent or child, the pain of losing a job or failing a class. It doesn't always keep us from the real horrors that life can inflict on us—the abuse, the betrayal, the unimaginable anguish that, for whatever reason, sometimes we have to deal with. But faith can save us from the mortal blow, the fire that would otherwise consume us. Our faith protects us when no one and nothing else can.

And it can do something else, too: with our faith, we can fly. We can look upon our worldly cares from a new, clearer vantage point. With faith, we can feel the breath of a greater power lift us, push us forward, and carry us home.

## THE COWL OF SALVATION

Batman's cowl offers Bruce Wayne some serious cranial protection, but the pointy-eared helmet does more than that. In *The Dark Knight*, Bruce Wayne equips it with a form of sonar, allowing him to detect objects in the dark. In the comics, it's also equipped with night-vision lenses and a special communications system that allows him to issue voice commands to various bat-gadgets. Presumably, he could tell the Batmobile to turn on its heated seats in advance of his coming if it's a particularly cold day in Gotham.

It's hard to overstate the importance of salvation for most Christians. It is the ultimate afterlife protection—a helmet that ensures that your motorcycle ride into the Great Beyond won't end badly. But like Batman's cowl, it offers some additional benefits to believers. Because they feel such security in their ultimate fate, Christians can experience the world a little more fully now as well. "Finding God does not mean building a house in a land of no storms," an anonymous believer once said, "but building a house that no storm can destroy." When we have that sort of security, it gives us the freedom to be bold and adventurous—hopefully for God's sake. Look at some of the heroes of our faith, and we see lives built of courage. Because they felt safe in their faith, they lived without fear. The annals of Christianity are filled with saints and martyrs who lived like this—as if they would live forever. Why? Because they knew they would, long after their mortal bodies had expired.

I have a hard time living without fear, even in the simplest matters. I'm a worrier by nature, and it's hard for me to trust in my helmet sometimes. *What happens if I lose my job?* I think to myself. *What happens if our roof springs a leak? What happens if . . . ? What happens when . . . ?*

But then when the "what happens" happens, a certain clarity settles. My fears have materialized, and yet I still stand. I still breathe. I still live. And more than that, I realize that these huge fears of mine weren't all that fearsome after all. It's in these moments when some cynics might say that God deserted me that I paradoxically remember that God's in control. That I'm in his hands. That whether I have a job or can afford to fix the roof or send my kids to college or have a potentially serious medical condition, my God is watching over me. He cares for me. And I feel *safe*—even if the world would tell me I'm not safe at all. When I'm forced to depend on God—when I have no other choice—that's when I feel the peace and the strength of his love and goodness and salvation.

In these moments, the clarity of that safety comes upon me like the strike of a bell. No longer is my attention sapped by worry. No longer do I waste my time wringing my hands ineffectively. I have to act, and so I do. It's too bad that I so often have to be pushed into this clarity. I wish that I could retain that sense of salvation all the time. I think it's that ability to emotionally embrace salvation—to trust the helmet—that gives Christianity its world-changing power. When we're not worried about our own safety, it turns us bold. Fearless. We become free to be the avatars of Christ that we're called to be. Our salvation allows us to see the world for what it is, not veiled by our own worries and cares. It gives us the power to hear the cries of others, which are so often drowned out by our own wimpy whines.

Salvation doesn't give believers the powers of sonar, but it can give us all a little more clarity—not so much as to what we can expect after this life (which, golden roads and pearly gates aside, is still a marvelous mystery), but what we're to be about in this one.

## THE BATARANGS OF THE SPIRIT

In spite of his aversion to firearms, Batman totes lots of weapons around, from gas pellets to nonlethal concussion grenades. But his most famous offensive tool is the stylish, versatile batarang, a bat-shaped piece of metal Batman hurls through the air to slow or stop evildoers. According to Beatty's *Ultimate Guide*, the Dark Knight has one for every occasion. Some are thrown like Frisbees, others like knives. One is equipped with a remote-controlled steering device, so the thing can chase a terrified villain like a tiny heat-seeking missile or even cut him off at the pass. Some have blunt edges, perfectly suited to inflict a quick thwack on the back of the head. Others have their metal edges honed to paper-thin sharpness or beveled to make a serrated cutting surface. Some are huge, intimidating hunks of metal, while others are tiny, the equivalent of ninja throwing stars, and many are hinged at the center so Batman can store them comfortably in his utility belt.

But as varied as they are, they all share one important trait: in true boomerang style, they can slice through the air to their target and, if all goes well (and they're not sticking in a villainous sleeve), flutter right back to Batman's hand.

In some ways, I think that makes Batman's batarang perhaps even more fitting an allegorical instrument than Paul's original sword.

While the image of a sword does convey both the power and even metaphorical lethality of the Spirit or the Word of God—both Christians and non-Christians can be cut to the quick by what we read in the Bible—the batarang speaks to its versatility. There is a book for every mood, a passage for every problem. While I'm not one to believe the Bible contains a clear, step-by-step blueprint for our lives—much of the book's beauty comes from its awesome mystery—I do think God designed it to teach us, to warn us, to feed our souls, and to foster our being, encouraging us in surprising ways. It's full of advice, of course, but it's loaded with poetry and history and imagery and, if I may be frank, some troubling passages that may challenge our faith more than build it. And yet the Bible embraces it all. We can struggle with doubt in Ecclesiastes, cry in despair in Psalms, curl up at the feet of Jesus in Luke. It can offer pragmatic advice or dive into fevered mystery. It can be blunt. It can cut us to the bone. It can thwack us upside the head or follow us wherever we go. It corrects and comforts, and we must never be without it.

## TOOLS IN A BETTER HAND

I could go on. Batman has more weapons than North Korea, more instruments than the New York Philharmonic. The Daytona 500 sports less power than the Batcave, what with all the planes, boats, helicopters, cars, and motorcycles down there. We could spend a full chapter on the Batmobile alone— though I'd be at a loss to tie the thing to a biblical symbol. Elijah's chariot, perhaps? The wheels of Ezekiel?

But for all of Batman's technological tools and toys, giz-mos and gadgets, his most amazing instrument is his own being: his mind, body, and spirit.

In the Batman epic *No Man's Land*, Gotham City has been abandoned, quarantined from the rest of the United States. Ravaged by plague and earthquake, Gotham has been declared an irredeemable mess by the government, which simply shut the place down.

But not everyone left. Some were too poor, too crazy, or too tied to this imperfect city to vacate. So in the aftermath of the government's decision, Gotham has become a petty fiefdom, with sections of the city ruled by warlords both familiar and new. It's a primitive city now: no gas stations, no electricity, certainly no thriving social media. The only "hot spots" are the burning offices and the only hashtags are those spray-painted on apartment-house bricks.

Batman is there, though, trying to bring a semblance of order to this chaotic world. But it's a world where many of his technological tools are useless. When he asks Barbara Gordon, daughter of the commissioner and a longtime high-tech helper of his, for some information tracking down a petty crimelord, she tells him she has no help to give. "I can't hack his computers because he doesn't have computers," she says. "I can't tap his phones because there are no phones. I can't even get second or third-hand information because the guns keep everyone away."

Batman, for once, is as blind as a bat.

"She made me realize how dependent I too had become on technology," he thinks as he walks through Gotham's inky black streets. "I'd gotten so used to databases and quick answers that it took me a moment to remember that my finest, most reliable computer was right here with me. My brain. To use it, all I had to do was think."

Batman doesn't just use instruments. He *is* one in the hands of a cause, perhaps in the hands of God.

Earlier we saw how Bruce Wayne became Batman through tragedy, time, and a whole lot of teachers. But becoming Batman is the easy part. The real trick is to *be* Batman, and to be an effective one at that. It's not easy. And you can forget the perks. Most of us would give up the job within a week—assuming, of course, we survived long enough to quit. Batman's been at it for decades.

"He doesn't have any superpowers except for his extra-ordinary capacity for self-discipline," Christopher Nolan says in *Batman Unmasked*.

We understand instinctively that Batman is more than the sum of his tools. Yes, he was made to be Batman, but he made himself, too, molding his mind and honing his talents to better serve Gotham and its people. He works incessantly at improving himself, in mind and body, as he upgrades his armor and equipment. The Batman of 2012 doesn't drive his '60s-era Batmobile or make do with his '50s-era fashion. And he is constantly trying to improve himself for his calling, his sacred quest. He reforges himself year after year, growing stronger with each trip through the fire.

He's a formidable man, undoubtedly. Through talent, work, and a whole lot of money, Batman has become a great instrument in the hands of a noble cause.

But really, what makes him great? What sets him apart? We know it's not his batsuit or secret laboratory. But is it his smarts? His strength? His skill?

No. His greatness is found in a simple kernel of humility: he's built himself for a purpose, just as a blacksmith might cast a hammer or forge a sword. He's serving something greater than himself. And he sacrifices all in that service.

For Christians, that's where Batman's real example lies—not in his weaponry (which we could never afford) or his ability (which we could never duplicate). It is in his willingness to serve.

When we look through the Bible, we see very few Batman-like characters. Most of our biblical heroes were poor. Many were weak. All, save Jesus, had flaws. What they shared, though, was a desire to serve, to be a tool in the hands of God, come what may. And when we learn about more modern-day saints and martyrs—the Mother Teresas, the Dietrich Bonhoeffers, the inner-city servants who minister to crack addicts, the social workers who help unwed mothers—they often brush away any thought that they might be heroes. They talk about serving or being the hands and feet of God. They want to be an instrument for Christ. A tool.

"When Christ calls a man, he bids him come and die," Bonhoeffer writes in *The Cost of Discipleship*. Sometimes that might mean to literally die, as Bonhoeffer did. For most of us, the sacrifice is not so dramatic but is no less intimidating. He bids us die to ourselves, to serve, to become a tool. For if we submit to God's will, if we become more nail than carpenter, more clay than potter, we can set aside our measly work and help God make something much more worthy: we can help make a better world.

## Chapter 7

# PARTNERS

*When you're down and troubled,*
*and you need some loving care,*
*And nothin', nothin' is going right,*
*Close your eyes and think of me and soon*
*I will be there,*
*To brighten up even your darkest night.*
—Carole King

**WHEN I WAS A CHILD,** the Batman I knew never worked alone. He was part of a set: Wherever Batman went, Robin the Boy Wonder was sure to follow—tagging along like the little brother Batman couldn't shake and, frankly, didn't want to. They were known as the Dynamic Duo, and while there was no doubt as to who the junior partner was, Robin was no ancillary add-on—a bonus superhero tossed in like a bargain-bin remainder. The Batman I grew up with needed him. Whenever someone shot at Bats from behind, Robin was there to shout a word of warning. Whenever the Dark Knight found himself imprisoned in some evildoer's lair, Robin found a way to free him. While DC, figuring an adolescent protagonist would appeal to the comic's adolescent readers, initially added the Boy Wonder to the comics to goose sales, it was an act of kindness, too: Batman, not having the godlike abilities of some of his fellow superheroes, needed more help than they did. He needed a friend. And so his creators gave him one.

It's a little strange for us to think of Batman as a social superhero these days since Christopher Nolan's Batman doesn't play well with others. He seems, in fact, the ultimate loner—an embodiment of solitude, wrapped in mystery and silence. And as if to emphasize his disdain for company, he slaps a mask on every night, a cowl to hide not just who he is but what he's thinking and feeling. It obscures not just his face but his soul, transforming him into that urban spectral myth he always intended Batman to be. Nothing says "Don't bother me!" like a mask covering three-fourths of your face. To look at Batman today, it's a little crazy to think this dark, menacing character who relies on shadow would ever be joined on his nightly rounds by some wisecracking kid wearing a red tunic and canary-yellow cape.

It's yet another dichotomy in the character of Batman. It's hard to reconcile that he's both a misanthropic loner *and* the most social of superheroes. But you've come so far already on this journey, so I'm sure you're game to try.

## THE LONE STRANGER

The solitary hero stands at the core of Batman's original character. Indeed, Nolan's Batman—the forbidding loner whose expression of choice is the glower—stays pretty true to the character of the Batman originally drawn by Bob Kane and Bill Finger in 1939. In those dark days before World War II, when America was still struggling through the Great Depression, Kane and Finger's solitary vigilante seemed to fit the national mood.

But then, we've always had a yen for lone heroes.

Instinctively we understand that being a hero can be lonely work. Folks become heroes by doing things that other people wouldn't dare to do. It's hard to stand up for our beliefs and ideals, to thumb our noses at the powers that be. If it were easy, everybody would be doing it. And if everybody did it, it'd be easy. It's no big deal to say you're in favor of civil rights for all Americans in the 2010s. But the folks who dared say such a thing in downtown Atlanta or Montgomery in the 1950s—well, they were heroes indeed. That's why courage and bravery and tenacity are such critical ingredients when it comes to making a hero. It's an inherently dangerous pro-fession, and chances are if you aspire to be a hero, you'll be spending some significant time feeling a little isolated. Frankly, if you don't feel alone sometimes, you're probably doing it wrong.

Don't believe me? Dust off your Bible and look at the heroes therein. Very often they seem to be isolated from their peers, set apart from the rest. Lot and his family clearly didn't fit in well with the folks of Sodom (Genesis 19:1-29). Judah, when he volunteered to become a slave in a foreign land in exchange for his younger brother, must have felt very alone (Genesis 44:33). Moses, even as he was leading the whole nation of Israel out of Egypt, seemed to always be on his own solitary journey too, taking the brave walk up the slopes of Sinai alone to retrieve the Ten Commandments (Exodus 19:20-22) or chatting with God one-on-one in the Tent of Meeting (Exodus 33:8-11). Jesus suffered and died alone, betrayed and abandoned by his closest friends and companions. As Christians, we understand that sometimes our call will lead us into some pretty lonely places.

And the theme of the lone man (or woman) standing against injustice persists. The solitary sheriff standing on a tumbleweed-strewn street, facing the black-hatted bad guy in a mano a mano shoot-out; the swashbuckling space captain ready to take on the evil minions of the planet Zib with just his trusty laser blaster and some derring-do. We love our John Waynes, our Indiana Joneses, our Jack Bauers, our Harry Potters . . . our superheroes. And while most of these characters have friends and associates to help them on their way, they always face their biggest challenges alone.

As you can see, Batman isn't alone in his loneliness. He's just more aggressive about it.

Batman, according to many modern narratives, eschews friendship as an impractical entanglement. In *Knightfall*, he largely rejects help from Robin and others to take all the risks himself. In the comic arc *Batman: Hush*, we learn he has difficulty bonding with others as a momentarily reformed Catwoman finds out during a heart-to-heart with the Caped Crusader.

"I . . . I am not very good at this," he says. "Having friends. Partners. It all ends in betrayal and death. If I ever could do it, then I lost it the night my parents were murdered."

But Catwoman sees through the facade.

"Tell that to Nightwing. Robin. Oracle," she says, rattling off some of Batman's more prominent partners and friends. "Do I need to go on?"

Batman—even modern, moody, sullen, solitary Batman—needs people, though he sometimes forgets it himself. And that need for companionship, community, and friendship is also deeply biblical.

## A CRAVING FOR COMPANY

Jesus, as we've seen, is something of a solitary hero. He was, as illustrated by his title "Son of God," set apart from his peers, different in a way that was apparent to anyone who met him. And in the climax of his story, he seemed very much alone, deserted by his disciples even as he suffered and died.

But while Jesus performed his greatest act by himself, his whole earthly ministry was about people. It's pretty obvious throughout the Gospels that he loved people, and he loved being with them. He was always teaching them or eating with them or healing them or just chatting with them. And on that fateful night before his crucifixion, he begged his friends to stay up with him, to keep him company. He made it pretty clear that the Christian life is one to be lived in community. "Where two or three gather together as my followers," he says in Matthew 18:20, "I am there among them." And when Jesus sent his disciples and followers to spread his message throughout Judea, he asked them to go in pairs (Luke 10:1). Other religions have their solitary sages and reticent mystics, and even Christianity has spawned its share of hermits. But God designed us to enjoy each other's company. We work better together.

So even though Batman was designed as a loner from the get-go, he also serves as a cautionary tale for what can happen when we spend *too* much of our time without some outside influence.

In Batman's early days—before Robin, before Alfred, and before Commissioner Gordon gave a rip—the Dark Knight sometimes devolved from merely brooding to positively disturbing. Our gloomy hero was liable to become a crank in a cape, perhaps prone to throw batarangs at the neighbor kids just out of pique. "The thing that bothered me was that Batman didn't have anyone to talk to," said original Batman artist Bill Finger in *Batman: The Complete History*. And apparently it bothered Batman, too.

In "The Spies," published in March 1940, Batman seems particularly peevish. He spends much of the episode talking to himself (after all, he doesn't have anyone else to chat with). And when he comes across another human being—even if it's a nefarious killer—he seems so relieved to have someone to talk with that he overdoes it.

"You don't look at all like Turg without your gray wig, your phoney mustache. and glasses off!" he says. "I had a hunch you were the 'Head' [the story's mysterious villain] when you didn't show up to-night! So the distinguished Count Grutt is really a foreign agent!" Count Grutt, by comparison, is far less verbose—perhaps because Batman won't stop talking. "Fool!" Grutt finally hollers, shortly before he impales himself on his own sword.

Batman wasn't all that sorry to see him go, rather out of character from the Dark Knight we know today. "It is better that he should die!" Batman tells us.

All of which makes him sound a little like me if *I'm* alone for too long. Lock me away for a couple of weeks—or even *days*—and I'm liable to start talking to myself and wishing ill on all manner of people. Being around others makes us better, I believe—or at the very least, more coherent.

The very next month, not wanting Batman to devolve into a muscle-bound, 1940s version of *The Simpsons's* crazy cat lady, DC brought Robin into the picture. And he wasn't the only friend to arrive on the scene over the years. Gotham these days teems with Batman's colleagues, confidants, and fellows. Not *buddies*, mind you—pals to play video games or grill hamburgers with. These aren't fair-weather or Facebook friends. Batman has very few of those. No, the people Batman allows into his life are allies who'd come to his aid at 3 a.m., individuals who would risk their careers, their well-being, even their lives to help him—perhaps because they know he'd do the same for them.

"You know, for a loner, you certainly have yourself a lot of strings," Catwoman tells Batman in *Hush*. She's right. And those strings extend into the realm of cinema—even into Christopher Nolan's exercises, where Gotham is a dark and lonely place and Robin is nowhere to be found.

Like Batman, we *need* friends, associates, and confidants too. We *need* people we can trust to care about us, to help us, to give us guidance, and to keep us on the right track. If we're going to be heroes in this world—if we're going to be the sort of people God intends for us to be—we'll need help. And Batman, in choosing his friends and partners, shows us how it's done. They give him support, care, and even love, after a fashion. They advise him, guide him, and, if need be, give him a kick in the rear. And a few of them have even seen behind the mask.

## ALFRED

In the modern Batman narrative, Alfred Pennyworth has known and cared for Bruce Wayne for, well, forever. As the Wayne family valet, he likely slapped Band-Aids on Bruce's scraped knees when he was just a boy and probably made him peanut butter and jelly sandwiches to take to school.

But after Bruce's parents died, we get a sense that caring for "Master Wayne," as he calls him, grew far more difficult. In *Batman Begins*, Bruce returns from college sullen and bitter, ready to chuck his father's legacy and trash the family mansion in a postadolescent tantrum. "This place is a mausoleum," Bruce blusters. "If I have my way, I'll pull the . . . thing down, brick by brick."

"This house, Master Wayne, has sheltered six generations of your family," Alfred reminds him, but Bruce can't understand why Alfred cares so much.

"It's not your family," he says.

Alfred explains why he has good reason to care. "A good man once made me responsible for what was most precious to him in the whole world," Alfred says. And for Alfred, that responsibility only ends when one of them dies.

It's only fitting, then, that Alfred (in the movies) was allowed behind Batman's mask from the very beginning. Indeed, he was instrumental in bringing Batman about: helping spelunk the Batcave, ordering Batman's cowls, and even coaching Bruce on the fine art of billionaire playboymanship.

"What does someone like me do?" Bruce asks in *Batman Begins*.

"Drive sports cars, date movie stars, buy things that are not for sale," Alfred says. "Who knows, Master Wayne? You start pretending to have fun, you might even have a little by accident."

But Alfred's role in creating Batman is nothing compared to what it takes to keep the legend going. At times in the comics, he assists the Dark Knight directly, venturing into Gotham's gloomy streets in disguise as a distraction or a spy. At others, he's called to defend Bruce Wayne's home, reputation, and alter ego. And when Batman springs a leak, Alfred's the one most likely to patch him up.

"I bet you have to do this pretty often?" Catwoman asks in *Hush* as Alfred lays a network of stitches on Batman's shoulder.

"No," Batman mumbles.

"Constantly," Alfred says, pulling the thread tight.

Whatever his wages, Alfred's underpaid. But does Alfred ever scour job websites, see if maybe Tony Stark needs a valet? No. As far as we can tell, Alfred never even takes a day off. He exemplifies a near-biblical model of servitude, caring for his master day after day, week after week, year after year.

"Alfred? Have you ever regretted your life here?" Bruce asks his faithful manservant in 1997's *Batman & Robin*.

"Looking after heroes?" Alfred responds. "No, sir."

"Well," Bruce says. "Not all heroes wear masks."

He's right. Because Alfred himself is a hero—one from whom Batman could learn a thing or two. He may not have the physical ability of his master (though Christopher Nolan's Alfred isn't one to be trifled with) or a mind as finely honed for detection (though in his 1940s comic book days, he considered himself an amateur sleuth). But he never loses sight of his duties nor falters in what he knows to be right. And if that sense of right and wrong clashes with the Caped Crusader, so be it. Alfred may be in the employ of Bruce Wayne, but that doesn't stop the valet from talking to Master Bruce like a wayward schoolboy when the need arises.

More than the mansion or the name, Alfred is Bruce Wayne's link to his father's goodness and his family's generous heritage. Alfred reminds Bruce not only who he is but who he's *supposed* to be and who he *can* be. Alfred desperately wants to see the best in Bruce—the possibilities, the promise. He *believes* in him. And perhaps that, more than Alfred's British wit or dexterity with a sewing kit, makes Batman possible.

We all could use someone like Alfred. Not Alfred the paid valet or Alfred the impromptu paramedic, but Alfred the friend. We need someone to believe in us. That doesn't mean they'll be blind to our faults. If they're close to us, they'll see us at our worst sometimes, when we're peevish, sullen, angry, or lost. But they'll find a way to look past all that and see, maybe a little dimly, the person we want to be—and can be, with a little help. They see us a little like God sees us, our actual and potential standing hand in hand. When we fall apart, they help put us back together. When we go astray, they give us a nudge—sometimes a kick—in the right direction.

And like Alfred, they're always underpaid.

Not everyone finds an Alfred. Not everyone gets the joy of *being* an Alfred. If you have, you should drop to your knees right now (after sliding a bookmark here, of course) and thank God for his goodness, because relationships like these are gifts we don't deserve. If I ever begin to doubt God's overwhelming, almost outlandish goodness, I only have to remember the folks he's brought into my life at my most critical moments. Without them, I can only assume I'd be destitute or dead. And I remember Jesus, too—how he came as a servant, how he sees the worst of us and yet believes the best of us. And while sometimes the people in our lives can come and go for one reason or another, he will always be at our side.

"I wouldn't presume to tell you what to do with your past, sir," Alfred tells Bruce in *Batman Begins* when Bruce gets back from college and fumes about tearing down the mansion "brick by brick." "Just know that there are those of us who care about what you do with your future."

"Haven't given up on me yet?" Bruce asks.

Alfred smiles.

"Never."

## LUCIUS FOX

As nigh-invincible as Batman is, he still hasn't found a way to vanquish time to his liking. Granted, he's markedly efficient with it, able to prowl Gotham's rooftops and still land in the tabloids as the city's most charismatic and colorful businessman. But between crime fighting and charity galas, Bruce/Batman has very little time to run Wayne Enterprises, the thing that makes both possible.

For that, Batman turns to Lucius Fox, as savvy a business partner as any superhero might hope for.

Lucius's backstory differs quite a bit between the comics and Christopher Nolan's movies. In print, Lucius is a business prodigy, a magna cum laude graduate of Morton Business School who's regularly wooed by Fortune 500 types. In the films, Mr. Fox was a former Wayne Enterprises board member, exiled to the company's basement before Bruce Wayne made him CEO. But one thing Lucius boasts in both media: ample smarts.

Good thing, too, because Lucius's gig demands that he stay on his toes.

In *Batman Begins*, Bruce and Lucius forge a friendship based on mutual interest, specifically Wayne Enterprises' applied science division. Bruce needs some high-tech gadgetry to use on his nocturnal outings. Lucius holds the keys to warehouses full of exotic armor and weaponry, and he's happy to loan it out—to the right person.

"Mr. Wayne, the way I see it, all this stuff is yours anyway," Lucius tells him.

But their relationship develops far beyond mere techno-trading. When Batman's stricken by one of Scarecrow's terrifying hallucinogens, Alfred calls Lucius for help—and in so doing reveals that Bruce and Batman are one. Lucius responds by developing an antidote for the hallucinogen through some impressive chemistry.

"I analyzed your blood, isolating the receptor compounds and the protein-based catalyst," he tells a still-mending Bruce.

"Am I meant to understand any of that?"

"Not at all; I just wanted you to know how hard it was."

From then on, Lucius isn't just CEO of Wayne Enterprises but a board member for Batman, Inc. He keeps the hero supplied with equipment, smoothing over the accounting irregularities as best he can. And when Batman needs some help apprehending a skittish corporate criminal from a foreign country, as happened in *The Dark Knight*, Lucius does what he can. In the same film, the businessman even tries to protect Batman from a Wayne Enterprises accountant who found some discrepancies in the company's R&D division and speculates that Mr. Wayne and Batman may be one and the same.

"Let me get this straight," Lucius says to the accountant. "You think that your client, one of the wealthiest, most powerful men in the world, is secretly a vigilante who spends his nights beating criminals to a pulp with his bare hands, and your plan is to blackmail this person?" Lucius lets his words skate around in the man's brain for a bit. And then, with an air of dismissal, he says, "Good luck."

But while Lucius may cook the books for Bruce (it is, as Lucius would tell you, Wayne's company), there are some things he doesn't like to do for his powerful benefactor. In *The Dark Knight*, when Bruce builds a Gotham-wide spy network by co-opting the city's cell phones—a last-ditch effort to catch the Joker—Lucius balks.

"This is too much power for one person," he tells Batman.

"That's why I gave it to you," Batman says. "Only you can use it."

Even then, Lucius is distrustful. He sees the technology as something like Sauron's ring from J. R. R. Tolkien's Middle Earth: a tool too dangerous, too inherently corrupting to use. He finally acquiesces, telling Batman he'll help him this one last time. But when the crisis is through, Lucius warns, he'll turn in his resignation.

It's with relief, then, that Lucius learns that Batman's network self-destructs the minute he signs off. The technological ring has been thrown into Mount Doom.

In choosing Lucius to handle this awesome technology, Batman made a pretty wise choice: Batman trusted Lucius—more than he trusted himself, perhaps.

By now we know something about Batman's darker inclinations; we know that he's not entirely pure, entirely true. And while Lucius is surely flawed—prone to stumble and fall just like the rest of us—Batman trusts him to resist some temptations that he himself might not. And that just makes sense, really: while Batman skulks in the shadows and has grown accustomed to smudged states of gray, Lucius operates in the sunlight. The lines between light and dark, right and wrong are sharper to his less-jaded eye. Lucius knows what Batman's trying to do in the city, and he supports it. But if Batman begins to drift into darkness, to slip into zealotry like Ra's al Ghul or despair like Two-Face, Lucius will either stop that drift or leave. He won't be a party to Batman's fall from grace.

To put it another way, Alfred believes in Bruce Wayne. Lucius believes in *Batman*—the myth, not the man; the hero, not the human behind the mask. Yes, he has great regard for Bruce Wayne, but he's in this game only as long as Batman is doing what he's supposed to do.

Sometimes we'd like to think our friends should be always accepting, always forgiving. "They like me for who I am," we like to say. But what if we're being jerks? What if we're drifting into areas that might hurt ourselves or others?

The Bible is loaded with exhortations to forgive, and we should. But forgiveness implies some sort of repentance first, and the Bible also tells us that we need to speak truth in love. It's not a comfortable thing to do. I can't imagine Lucius Fox was feeling particularly buoyant when he threatened to resign. But sometimes we have to do it. And sometimes our friends have to do it to us, because there are times we don't know when we're going astray, when we're drinking too much or not spending enough time with our families or stepping over ethical boundaries at school or work. That's the thing about evil: we're not whisked over to the dark side all at once, but rather step by step, taking us into environs just a little grayer, a little darker. We need people to drag us back into the sunlight.

In Matthew 18, Jesus actually tells us what to do if someone close to us—a fellow Christian—sins against us. We're to talk with that person one-on-one at first. If that doesn't work, we should bring in a few others who have seen the same problem—an intervention of sorts. Then, if there's still no repentance, Jesus tells us to take it to "the church," a move hardly anyone seems to make these days. After all this, if our wayward friend is determined to stay wayward, Jesus tells us to do one final, impossibly hard thing: turn away from him or her.

Lucius obviously skipped a few of Jesus' steps in there, and the circumstances were different. But when Lucius felt that Batman was wandering unapologetically into the darkness, he threatened to turn away. And he illustrates a hard fact about friendship: It's not always about accepting who we are and seeing the best in us, like Alfred. It's about making us better, like Lucius tries to do with Bruce. And sometimes it's about doing a little bit of both.

## JIM GORDON

If Alfred is loving and Lucius is virtuous, Jim Gordon (known for most of Batman's tenure as Commissioner Gordon) is just plain good. Like Batman, he despises corruption and fights Gotham's underworld with seemingly inexhaustible energy. But Gordon wages his battles inside the system, not outside the lines. This makes him, in my eyes, a better man than Batman: his motives are clearer, his methods cleaner. Perhaps it shouldn't surprise us that when Gordon and Batman arrive in Gotham, they find themselves on different teams.

"Commissioner Loeb set up a massive task force to catch

you," Gordon, then a sergeant, tells Batman in *Batman Begins*. "He thinks you're dangerous."

"What do you think?" Batman asks him.

"I think you're trying to help," Gordon admits, but when he turns to face him, Batman's gone.

"But," Gordon sighs to himself, "I've been wrong before."

In Frank Miller and David Mazzucchelli's *Batman: Year One*, Gordon (a lieutenant) heads up the city's task force to nab Batman, and much of the graphic novel centers around the cat-and-bat chase between Gotham's masked magnate and its one incorruptible police officer. But even though his orders are clear, Gordon struggles with a grudging admiration for his lawbreaking target, who by all appearances is acting like one of the good guys.

"He's a criminal," Gordon thinks, sitting at the edge of his bed holding his handgun. "I'm a cop. It's that simple. But—but I'm a cop in a city where the mayor and the commissioner of police use cops as hired killers. . . . He saved that old woman. He saved that cat. . . . The hunk of metal in my hands is heavier than ever."

In *Year One*, Gordon aligns himself with Batman after the hero, sans cape, dressed only in a business suit, dives into a murky river to save Gordon's infant son. Comforting his baby boy, Gordon, glasses lost somewhere on the road, looks into Batman's—into Bruce Wayne's—eyes as the rain pounds down and says, "You know, I'm practically blind without my glasses. Sirens coming. You'd better go."

Gordon already knew that Batman, whoever he was, had to be incredibly wealthy. He had already questioned Bruce

Wayne. Did Gordon recognize his son's rescuer for who he was? Miller and Mazzucchelli allow Gordon's words to be accepted as truth—though if Gordon were cross-examined, perhaps we'd learn differently.

In the subsequent decades, Batman and Gordon fight for Gotham's soul together, two knights standing in unison, shield to sword. They're friends now, brothers in arms, each sharing the same goals even as they take different paths to reach them.

But as close as Gordon is to Batman, he can't and won't allow the vigilante to stray too far from the light. When Batman edges close to breaking his code—his "one rule," as he says in *The Dark Knight*—Gordon's often around to stop him from doing something he'll regret.

In *Hush*, Batman confronts the Joker yet again. The Harlequin of Hate has already killed Jason Todd, who served as Robin for a time. He's shot Barbara Gordon, the commissioner's daughter, paralyzing her from the waist down. Now the Joker has a gun in his hand again, and he's standing over the corpse of Batman's closest childhood friend, a man who just recently saved Bruce Wayne's life.

Batman snaps.

He begins beating Joker under Gotham's ever-weeping skies. Soon, Joker's white face is shellacked with blood. "I'm innocent," he protests. "It's just another lie," Batman thinks, slamming his nemesis into a wall. "Another lie to keep himself alive. . . . There is nothing I can do to him that would cause him the agony that he has brought upon others. But I can come close."

A shot cracks behind Batman and Joker. A bullet grazes Batman's arm.

"Stand up and put your hands in the air," Commissioner Gordon's voice booms through the rain.

Joker is vanquished, bleeding in the downpour. The battle now is between Batman and Gordon, between righteous anger and a higher calling.

"If Batman wanted to be a killer, he could have started a long time ago," Gordon says. "But, it's a line. On one side we believe in the law. On the other . . . Batman, if you cross that line—if you kill the Joker tonight—I will lead the hunt to bring you to justice. In the eyes of the law . . . in *my* eyes you'll be no different from him."

Batman looks down, blood coating his gauntlets. "How many more lives are we going to let him ruin?" Batman asks, like an angry teen or wayward child.

"I don't care," Gordon says. "I won't let him ruin yours."

The battle is over. The hero has won—the hero that is Commissioner Gordon.

There have been instances when Batman has held the commissioner back too, for the record. This is no one-sided relationship. Each has held the other accountable, forcing an adherence to the lofty ideals they both hold so dear.

How critical is it for all of us to have people hold us to our own standards? How crucial is it to be held accountable? We live at a time and in a place where we're sometimes told there is no right or wrong, there is no line to cross. Batman lives in such a world too. When Batman chose his friends and allies, he chose people who loved him, trusted him, and in a way accepted him for who he was. But more important, they all saw what he *wanted* to be—what he *could* be—and pushed him to see it too, even when Batman was too blind to see it himself.

Yes, Batman, the ultimate loner, has friends. He has, in Catwoman's words, "strings"—not to bind him but to hold him together, to help fasten him to the purpose to which he's committed his life.

He needs those strings. He needs people to support him and hold him to account. Life is too hard to live alone. And when we try to live a Christian life, the need for love and support is all the more important because the way forward is difficult. I think that's why many Christians place such a huge emphasis on having a relationship with God and with Jesus: we need not just his power or grace, but on some mystical level, we need his friendship, too.

Don't be fooled by the pretty pamphlets or late-night preachers. To be a Christian is to take the narrow road, a road often overgrown and indistinct, full of bumps and divots and rocks we've got to scramble over. There are so many opportunities to get lost or sidetracked. So it's good to have someone on the walk with us, someone to show us the way.

## Chapter 8

# STRUGGLE

*Ah me! How hard a thing it is to say*
*What was this forest savage, rough, and stern,*
*Which in the very thought renews the fear.*
—Dante, *Inferno*

**IT IS A DARK NIGHT** in a place that has known many. Harvey Dent, Gotham's district attorney, is missing. The Joker has been captured, and yet he smiles. Laughs. Taunts. And Batman, the city's shadowed hero, is about to lose it.

Batman holds the Joker by the collar against the interrogation room's bleached-bone walls, his forearm pressed against the Joker's neck. He could kill his adversary here, in a second, with a shove and a twist. The Joker's weak. He's in jail. Batman has him beaten. And yet Gotham's olive-haired jester is in complete control.

"There's only minutes left, so you're going to have to play my little game if you want to save one of *them*," he sneers in *The Dark Knight*.

"Them!" Batman gasps.

The Joker licks his lips. "For a while there, I thought you really were Dent, the way you threw yourself after her."

With a grunt and a heave, Batman throws the Joker on the interrogation table with a hollow, metallic thud, then grabs a chair and sticks it against the door—keeping Jim Gordon and the rest of Gotham out. In this tiny room, Batman is justice, vengeance, the angel of death. And yet the Joker laughs. He *laughs*. "Look at you go!" he giggles.

Batman grabs him by the hair and bashes his face into the interrogation window, sending spider veins across the glass. "Where are they!" Batman bellows, hitting him in the face. "Where are they!" Again, the gauntlet lands against the Joker's jaw.

And still the laughter spurts out of the villain like ketchup, bouncing against tile and glass to mock all Batman is and everything he stands for. It's laughter from the abyss, laughter from the void.

"You have nothing!" the Joker chortles. "Nothing to threaten me with! Nothing to do with all your strength!"

It's true. Batman, with all his power, is powerless. The Joker laughs. The world laughs. It is a dark night indeed in a place that has known many.

## A PEOPLE TO BE PITIED?

The Christian walk has its share of dark nights, when the world seems to laugh at us. We, who claim to be loved by the Designer of all things as his own sons and daughters . . . who say we know the purpose we were born for . . . who have the audacity to proclaim that we personally know the one who has the keys to everlasting life . . . we hear the void mock us. We, in our faith, claim power eternal and ageless victory. And yet there are moments when it feels like . . . nothing.

We can all suffer through times like these, I think. Sometimes we get angry with God for what we feel he has (or hasn't) done. Sometimes we just feel a great distance between us and him—a remove, like a lover disenchanted. Sometimes we may wonder whether he's listening to us at all. We wonder whether our faith is a sham, whether we might be, in the apostle Paul's words, a people "more to be pitied than anyone in the world" (1 Corinthians 15:19).

And part of what makes all this pain and suffering so galling is how unfair it seems. God, after all, has revealed his character and heart to us in the person of his Son, and he showed us his unfailing love with his Son's ultimate sacrifice. Why should we doubt? God has told us that he's all-knowing, all-loving. Why, then, would he allow us to suffer? It seems crazy to us. No wonder we get angry. No wonder we start to question.

But how do we get beyond our struggles? How do we move beyond our suffering? Is it possible to plow through all this pain and find purpose on the other end?

Of course. And once again, Batman can show us how.

In the scene from *The Dark Knight* recounted above, the Joker challenges Batman's makeshift faith in two ways—the two primary avenues in which our own faith is challenged. The first comes from outside Batman, the pain others inflict on him. The second comes from inside, the doubt he suffers not so much at the Joker's hands but through the Joker's intimations of Batman's own darkest dread. The Joker gives voice to Batman's ultimate fear: that Batman may be wrong (pitied above all people) and that the Harlequin of Hate really might be ahead of the curve.

## PAIN

We see—almost physically feel—Batman inflicting mountains of pain on the Joker during that interrogation scene in *The Dark Knight*, but it's nothing compared to the red-hot poker the villain jams into Batman's innards. He twists the hero's moment of triumph into defeat, revealing that he holds not just Harvey Dent but Rachel Dawes, Dent's fiancée and Bruce Wayne's true love (or, at least, as close to a true love as Bruce has ever had). Batman already saved Rachel's life once in the movie. How tragic, how *unfair* would it be to lose her now?

"Killing is making a choice," the Joker taunts. "Choose between one life or the other. Your friend, the district attorney, or his blushing bride to be."

Batman is confronted with the sort of loss and pain that all of us dread: the loss of someone close to us and the pain of feeling—fairly or no—that we could have done something to stop it.

We hate pain; we hate to suffer. And most of us will do almost anything to avoid it. I have a friend who after a particularly horrific trip to the dentist in her teens avoided seeing another one for fifteen years. My own daughter—now seventeen—still lives in apoplectic fear of getting a shot. I'm okay with dentists and vaccinations, but I act like a little baby if I get a papercut. And as horrible as the little dents and dings we all suffer physically can be, that stuff pales in comparison to the emotional horrors we must all grapple with at some points in our lives: disappointment, sickness, death. . . . If we live, we suffer; there's no getting around it. And some of us, I've observed but haven't quite reconciled, suffer more than others.

But pain is not a sin or a temptation or a state of mind; we can't pluck a villain from Batman's pantry of villainy and say, as we did with Catwoman or Scarecrow, "This one represents pain." Pain is inflicted *on* us, which means there's someone or something else doing the inflicting. Sometimes that someone is us. But very often our pain is a symptom of another evil or even sometimes another good. Pain can lead us—or more accurately, *drag* us, kicking and screaming most likely—to a better place, a sense of purpose or even a life of faith.

That said, it's the pain that comes *after* we've found purpose, *after* we've found a place in the palm of God, that's so horribly vexing.

## SUFFERING AFTER SALVATION . . .

Batman is clearly not a stranger to pain. He could probably write a doctoral thesis on the subject. He was spawned from the pain of losing his parents. He was shaped by the pain of not being able to make it right.

Bruce Wayne's transformation into Batman recalls many

people's conversion to Christianity: a realignment of values and purpose to something higher. If you've been a Christian for any length of time, chances are you've heard someone give his testimony—how awful his life was before he "met Jesus." "I was a pimp, a drug dealer, and a meth addict," he might have said, "living on the streets in Vegas, selling off my organs one by one for the next high. And then I met Jesus, and my whole life changed."

Pain can do us good. It can reset our instruments to follow a higher calling. It can lead us to Christ. It can change our lives. But you'd think that once the need for that resetting pain was gone and we were safely in the loving affections of our heavenly Father, we'd stop feeling so much pain, right? Things should get easier . . . shouldn't they?

If you read the wrong Christian pamphlets or listen to too many late-night preachers, you'll hear that they do. Even some of those sin-to-salvation testimonies can lead us to believe that life doesn't just get better, as in, "I'm really satisfied with the trajectory my life is on and the impact I'm making on other people," but it gets *better*, as in, "God blessed me with good health and a smokin' hot girlfriend and a winning lottery ticket. Now that I'm Christian, I can buy that BMW I've always wanted." If you've endured a handful of evangelistic-minded Christian movies, as I have, you'll know that most of them chronicle how horrible a person's life was before Christ entered it. And everything after the conversion is summed up with sunshine and violins and maybe a "he lived happily ever after" notation right before the credits roll.

Sometimes I think Christians can be guilty of selling their faith like a bait-and-switch scam. Because the truth is, not all people's lives get easier when they meet Jesus. In fact, they can get quite a bit harder. And so when we find ourselves on the other end of a baptism with all of life's problems still very much with us—and with maybe a host of others to boot—it's understandable that we feel a little let down. We're kids on Christmas morning who, instead of finding a Red Ryder BB gun underneath the tree, unwrap a snow shovel and are asked to use it on the driveway.

That sense of disappointment is reflected in Christopher Nolan's *The Dark Knight*. When the film opens, we at first see a city with just a wee bit more bounce in its stride—a city made better because of Batman. Criminals are awkwardly doing their dirty work in the broad daylight because they're worried about Gotham's winged wonder nabbing them at night. Ordinary citizens grow so inspired that they try to chip in, taking on the city's underworld with nothing more than tennis rackets and enthusiasm. Bruce Wayne's mysterious and mystical persona has made a difference. Bruce's life was changed. The city was changed.

And then came the Joker, toting his special formula for pain, and Gotham's faith shuddered. He kidnapped one of the city's self-made vigilantes and, before killing him, forced him into a mass-media humiliation, his final moments shown on TV.

"Are you the real Batman?" the Joker asks the man, bound and bruised.

"No," the man says.

"No?" the Joker gasps in mock surprise. "Then why do you dress up like him?" He grabs the man's mask and jiggles it in front of the camera like a marionette.

"Because he's a symbol that we don't have to be afraid of scum like you," the man spits out, spending what appears to be his last bit of mental and spiritual strength—a martyr making a last gesture before being led to the lions.

"Yeah, you *do*, Brian," the Joker tells him. "You really do. Yeah. So, you think Batman's made Gotham a better place? Hmm? Look at me. Look at me!" He turns the camera to his own face.

"You see? *This* is how crazy Batman's made Gotham! You want order in Gotham? Batman must take off his mask and turn himself in. Oh, and every day he doesn't, people will die. Starting tonight. I'm a man of my word."

Fear. Pain. Suffering. Sometimes when we make changes in our lives for the better, it doesn't make our lives better. Sometimes the struggles keep coming. Sometimes they get worse.

Some might say that in a universe backed by a just and loving God, Gotham would have been spared the Joker. Bruce Wayne would have been given full cosmic points for his transformation, and he and his favorite city would skip off, hand in metaphorical hand, into the sunset to live happily ever after—just like we'd see at the end of some Christian movies. But that doesn't happen here. And in light of this obvious miscarriage of justice, some might shake their fists at the heavens and demand of God why he'd let a good man suffer like this.

## THE PLOT THICKENS

Christianity's forebears weren't unmindful of suffering. While some modern preachers tell us that God will unfailingly reward those who are faithful to him, providing them with lives of comfort and wealth, the Bible itself offers a far more nuanced and difficult examination of God's blessings (or apparent lack thereof). In the Old Testament, the God-fearing faithful would lament their lot in poem and prose, sometimes screaming at God in their pain and anguish. In New Testament times, as martyrs began to mount, newly stamped Christians were well aware that life wasn't to be a trip to the circus (though some later became all too familiar with performing lions).

I'm no theologian, but even if I were, I doubt I could answer why people suffer like they sometimes do—why God allows so much misery in this world of ours. Lots of very wise and inspired men have considered and written about this "problem of pain." And while their theological and intellectual ruminations often make sense, they're still only abstract—cold comfort when we're in the throes of pain our-selves. Few of us much care about *why* people suffer when we're actually suffering. We just want it to stop. We want someone to *make* it stop. And when we're well aware that we serve a God who *could* stop it but for some reason doesn't, that hurts us all the more.

In the end, then, all our questioning comes to naught. We question, and the answer, in the form of another question, thunders back at us: "Do you still want to argue with the

Almighty? You are God's critic, but do you have the answers?"
(Job 40:2). God owes us no answers and often gives us none,
at least not in this lifetime. So if we want to keep following
the path we know to be right, we're left with only one course:
we must come to peace with our pain.

And to do that, for me it helps to remember that as much as
we'd like to be, we are not the sole authors of our lives. We are
characters on a stage already set for us in the midst of a plot we
don't fully understand and a finale we can't quite grasp. As we
play our parts and craft our lines, millions of other people are
doing the same thing—sometimes putting them at odds with
ours. And God orchestrates this fantastic, organically growing
epic—not writing the players' dialogue for them or forcing
them to do certain things, but somehow salting our actions
to ultimately reflect his own Spirit and breath and meaning.

"A man has control over many things in his life; he has
control over enough things to be the hero of a novel," writes
G. K. Chesterton in *Heretics*. "But if he had control over
everything, there would be so much hero that there would
be no novel."

Batman, I think, understands this simple truth. He's the
protagonist thrown into a plot not of his own choosing.
It's been that way from the beginning with him—from the
moment he watched his parents die in Crime Alley.

Batman didn't have control that fateful night. And in
*The Dark Knight*, he doesn't have control over the Joker, the
personification of chaos. In Batman's world, Joker happens.
Batman doesn't control Brian (his biggest fanboy imitator) or
Harvey Dent (an archenemy in the making) or Rachel Dawes

(the love of his life who keeps slipping through his fingers). If Batman did control them, he'd surely have forced them all to spend their foreseeable futures locked away in safe, gated communities (called Arkham Asylum, in the Joker's case), and there would be no story.

Chesterton tells us that we're not living in a scientific textbook but a romance, full of unlikely plot twists and jaw-dropping cliffhangers and, alas, moments of pain and suffering. Good stories, the stories we remember, test their heroes to the utmost; that's a big reason why we remember them. So why does it surprise us so much when our own stories have their share of strife? Why do we pound our fists and scream "foul" to the heavens? Our lives aren't really written in textbooks or treatises, but in stories. The universe isn't written solely in elements and atoms (though it's about those things too), but in words. "Let there be light!" God said in Genesis 1:3—light crafted not by hands or tools or a cosmic chemistry lab but with a sentence.

Our God is a storyteller. And the best stories often don't make sense to readers until the very end. The best we can do if we take part in such a story is plow through, page after page, and play our parts, moment to moment, as best we can.

And so Batman does. Every twist the Joker throws him demands a decision from the Dark Knight, a decision that will affect not only his story but other people's too. It's as if the Joker hisses, "Take off the mask and save some lives. Choose which life to save, Harvey Dent's or Rachel Dawes's. Choose your path. Choose your pain."

And so Batman does. Not without regret, not without

suffering, but without the tang of marring his own character. Batman stays true to himself, his story, and his purpose. He accepts the pain. He accepts the suffering. And in so doing he remains a hero. Why? Because that's what heroes do.

Rarely are heroes defined by their superpowers or their technogadgets. They don't set themselves apart by their strength or intelligence or abilities. Rather, it's by sheer tenacity: heroes push forward no matter the cost of doing what's right, through pain, through suffering, through heartbreak, through injustice. Just as we better understand the power of light when it's surrounded by darkness, so we better understand the quality of our heroes by how they persevere through pain. Without struggle, there can be no heroism. After all, we'd all do what was right if it were easy. It's doing what's right when things get tough that sets heroes apart.

But what happens if we're no longer sure what's right? What if we begin to question the validity of heroism itself?

## DOUBT

It's one thing to become angry with God. It's another to wonder whether there's a God with whom one can become angry. The Joker, in that bleak interrogation room, forces Batman to question whether his ethics, his code, and his life—a life given to a greater purpose—matter. The Joker wants the Dark Knight to ask the critical question: What if our morals really are a "bad joke?" What if the Joker has been right all along?

"The only sensible way to live in this world is without

rules," he says, "and tonight, you're going to break your one rule."

Literature's most compelling bad guys are so effective because they tap into a wellspring of doubt and desire, found in the darkest recesses of our own souls. They scare us because they understand us; or, more accurately, we understand them. The Joker is so repulsive in part because he's so compelling, even relatable. He's horribly vile, terribly wrong . . . and yet some of us, maybe many of us, are scared that his crazy logic makes sense.

Now, I'm not saying that the Joker could ever convince you to start stabbing people in the forehead with pencils or blow up ferries full of passengers. But the path he takes to get to his gleeful nihilism is remarkably straightforward and surprisingly short. His worldview is simple, logical, and coherent. He may be crazy, but his ethos is consistent.

The Joker begins with one basic assumption: the universe is a cold void, and anything in it is a product of chaotic chance. There is no reason behind it, no design. It is what it is, devoid of karma or compassion, with no greater substance within its vast folds to care how we spend our brief and accidental lives.

This, as you know, isn't an uncommon assumption, nor does it invariably lead to its adherents smearing white grease paint all over their faces. There are many, many people who believe in a godless universe, and the vast majority of them, from a worldly perspective, are decent, caring people.

But for the Joker, another assumption follows the first: a godless universe is also by its nature an amoral universe.

There can be no innate, overarching morality to which we're bound. Nothing is sacred because the sacred does not exist. There is no need to treat anything as if it were.

This is where many atheists and agnostics veer away from the Joker. Some contend that even without God there is still an inherent morality to which we're bound, an unwavering sense of good and evil. Others admit that such a concept is inherently impossible in a mindless cosmos, and so we as individuals and societies must craft our own morality to which we must then bind ourselves.

But the Joker questions the rationality of both stratagems. If the universe is without real purpose, then *we* are without real purpose. If the void is amoral, then *we* are amoral too. No sense in pretending we're something we're not, he figures. What good is "good" if we make it up as we go along? Why shouldn't each of us do exactly as we please? And if what pleases us involves destruction, murder, and copious amounts of hair dye, well, what's it to ya?

The Joker feels that his worldview is as good as anyone's; better, in fact, since it's more honest, more distilled. And he spreads the bad news like a fiery street preacher—using real fire, naturally. But the convert he most desires is Batman, and so he tries to chip away at the hero's apparent incorruptibility, his purpose nothing less than pulling the Bat off his lofty perch and down into the gutter with him.

And Batman, like it or not, is susceptible to the tug.

Pain isn't much of a deterrent for our Caped Crusader. Like the Joker in that interrogation room, he seems largely unmoved by it. He's dealt with pain all his life and accepts it as part of the job. But doubt—that's something else. At times Batman *does* wonder whether his sacrifices make a difference, whether his work has done any good. He wonders whether there's any purpose behind who he is or what he does.

"I've lost my way," Bruce Wayne confesses to Alfred in the year-long DC saga *No Man's Land*. "It's all gone gray, Alfred. The doubt and the confusion . . . I can't see the way any longer." Like Dante, Batman sometimes finds himself "within a forest dark, for the straightforward pathway had been lost." And that makes him exactly like us.

In the church I grew up in, having a "personal relationship with God" was a big deal, and church folks encouraged me to think of Jesus as my best friend. As we've read, there's a real validity to embracing Jesus as a companion; we need him in that way. But it's hard for a seven-year-old (or at least me as a seven-year-old) to get too companionable with someone you can't see, hear, or touch. I believed in Jesus, and I believed he cared for me, but I knew he wasn't the sort of guy I could explore the neighborhood, watch cartoons, or play tag with. A game of hide-and-seek with Jesus can be pretty frustrating.

And sometimes even now my relationship with God can feel like hide-and-seek, where God's always hiding and I'm always seeking. This relationship is *work*, and as noisy as our lives are these days, it can be hard to hear that quiet voice in which God so often talks.

That's the way it is with some of us, though how we react to this arrangement differs from person to person. Some, I think, really begin to question whether there's a God out there at all. That's not so much the case with me anymore (though it used to be). But I do find myself, more often than I'd care to admit, taking my faith for granted or pushing it to the side rather than setting it as a cornerstone for my whole way and being. I set aside the Bible to read the Internet, push away quiet time to dive into a new video game. That's the flip side of having an assurance that God is always there: it means he's *always there*, which means he becomes less of a priority and my time with him begins to get shoved into the out-of-the-way crevices of the day, week, or month. He becomes a facet of my life rather than the core of it.

When we marginalize our faith, our doubts creep in. We lose our way in the forest dark without a sense of who we are or what we should be about. I've learned this lesson more times than I care to admit. And I have a suspicion that I'll have to be taught it again before it sinks in for good.

Batman is not alone in his struggle. I am not alone in mine. Doubts are invariably a part of faith. The Bible is full of people who have expressed doubts or struggles or have questioned God's nature. And while we're told never to test God, there seems to be an understanding in the Bible that it's natural at times to question him. For someone like me, who's always full of impertinent questions, that's incredibly comforting. There's an assurance that God can handle the tough questions and loves us in spite of our doubts. But that doesn't make the questions any easier to answer or the doubts any simpler to dispel.

If you are right now living with serious doubts, I don't think a book on the spiritual parallels of a superhero—no matter how cool that superhero might be—will dispel them. But I hope it will encourage you to grapple with them instead of shoving them aside. Doubts, like pain, spring from different causes and ultimately have different remedies. For some, there's an intellectual hurdle to be overcome. For others, it's an emotional disconnect or distance from faith. For still others, it can be a willful rejection, a refusal to open their hearts to the wonder and reality of faith. I've wandered through all these forms of doubt (maybe most Christians have) and come out on the other side, faith intact.

And through my own struggles, here's the crux of what I've learned: faith is hard. And faith, when we see it manifested in others (or even in ourselves), doesn't always reflect the eternal beauty it should. And yet to believe and to worship is part of my being—no easier to eradicate from my body than my heart or lungs. It is at the core of everything I am, even if it's not always reflected in everything I do. It is the beginning and end of me, the reason for me. And the only way I can be truly myself is through faith.

It is the same with most of us, I think. It's why even in a world growing more secular by the year, more than 80 percent of us still believe in something. A recent study found that half of self-described atheists still pray. In the midst of all our doubts, all our skepticism, we know a deeper truth. We know. Somehow we feel it within us, the divine spark. It gives us hope and purpose. It makes us who we are.

And there's no better illustration of that than Batman.

In Grant Morrison and Dave McKean's creepy graphic novel *Arkham Asylum: A Serious House on Serious Earth*, the

Dark Knight plunges through a world of dreamlike insanity, run (naturally) by Joker himself. Its authors intended the piece to be a psychological and spiritual quest, a mythic journey to the underworld where Batman would face his deepest terrors and darkest doubts. And in the midst of this quest, he again takes on the characteristics of a storied knight, searching the darkness for a sacred, saving cup.

"Like Parsifal, I must confront the unreason that threatens me," he thinks, name-checking one of Arthur's knights most famous for his quest of the Holy Grail. "I must go alone into the Dark Tower. Without a backward glance. And face the dragon within."

He finds a dragon in the guise of the lizard-like Killer Croc, one of Batman's most notorious enemies (and, as Morrison notes, a symbol for "the Old Dragon in Revelations"). In the midst of the fight, Batman's inward doubts and struggles mirror the battering blows Batman absorbs at the hand of his (the) adversary. "There is nothing to hold onto," he churns, even as he grasps a ledge. "No anchor. Panic-stricken, I flee. I run blindly through the madhouse. And I cannot even pray. For I have no God."

It's a great depiction of who we are when we have no faith—unmoored not just from our God but from our own nature and purpose.

Then before him stands a statue of the archangel Michael, poised to skewer a monstrous serpent with a huge spear. Batman grabs the spear from the angel's hands and stabs the side of the dragon. Vanquished, the creature falls through a window and vanishes, like a dream.

Morrison intended Michael and his spear to represent reason, with which Batman skewered the assaulting chaos to return to form. And given Batman's status as such an ultra-reasonable superhero, the symbolism makes sense. But in the context of what we're talking about here, I think we can push the symbolism further.

The appearance of Michael, and Batman's taking up his spear, represents his return to purpose—and a return to faith. Since medieval times, Michael has long been associated with chivalry and its values (both France and England named orders in honor of the angel), and in many Christian circles today he's regarded as a patron saint of warriors. In John Milton's *Paradise Lost*, Michael led the forces of heaven against Satan's fallen, besting the Prince of Darkness in battle. How fitting, then—how resoundingly, poetically appropriate—that Michael (or at least a stone facsimile thereof) was on hand to help another warrior when he needed it most.

It's telling that Batman's return to purpose came not by reflection but by action. Christianity is, after all, a faith based on action. And while being active in our faith isn't a *cure* for doubt, it can come close. Comforting someone else can often help ease our own grief. Just as a good, long run can help us set aside the stress of school or work for a time and even help us put it all into perspective, so too can faithful spiritual activity change our view of God. To be active is a very Christian thing to do. While most world religions base their belief strictures on what their leaders said, Christianity is as much about what Jesus *did*. We're not supposed to spend all our time in solitude at the tops of mountains where we mull over the nature of God (though a little of that is good too). We're meant to act. We're members of an action-oriented faith, and as such we all have the potential to be . . . action heroes?

It is "only by living completely in this world that one learns to have faith," writes theologian and martyr Dietrich Bonhoeffer. "By this worldliness I mean living unreservedly in life's duties, problems, successes and failures. In so doing we throw ourselves completely into the arms of God, taking seriously, not our own sufferings, but those of God in the world. That, I think, is faith."

In that interrogation room, as the Joker twisted and tore into Batman with his diabolical games, Batman *acted* in the midst of his doubts, persevered through the pit of his pain. He pushed his own fears and struggles aside and again heeded the better call. After Batman initially runs to save Rachel, the girl he considers to be his one true love, I believe he changes his mind mid-course, determined instead to rescue Harvey Dent, Gotham's white knight. It was an excruciating choice, an unfair choice, but it was *a choice*. And in making it he set the needs of his city before his own. He abided by his code, affirming his purpose. Batman, through action, paid homage to his calling, as painful as it proved to be.

## Chapter 9

# SACRIFICE

*When Christ calls a man, he bids him come and die.*
—Dietrich Bonhoeffer, *The Cost of Discipleship*

**I'M TRYING TO LOSE** a pound or two. It's not a lot of weight, mind you—just enough to keep my buttons from flying off my jeans. I don't think I'll need to adopt a fad diet, like the grapefruit diet or the flavored-water diet or the all-the-air-you-can-eat diet. I'll just need to cut back a little here and there. Cull my junk food intake, maybe cut down on the pop I drink.

Which makes me wonder . . . why are those Oreos sitting by my elbow? What's that Mountain Dew doing by my computer monitor? Why am I reaching for one of those Oreos and stuffing it into my—

(Cue the sound of ravenous chewing.)

Clearly, I am not the best person to talk about sacrifice. While I'll tell you that I'd lay down my life for my wife (and even believe it myself), that doesn't keep me from rolling my eyes and muttering under my breath when she tells me to pick up some milk from the store. I'd give my kids anything to ensure that they're happy, healthy, and well-adjusted— unless it's my undivided attention when there's a Denver Broncos game on. I'd give my friends one of my kidneys if they asked for it, but I wouldn't give them the last slice of pizza if I was still kind of peckish.

And maybe I'm not all that unusual. As a species, I think we're big talkers when it comes to sacrifice but don't show a lot of follow-through. We say we'll cross oceans and deserts for those we love . . . just don't ask us to let the guy pass us in traffic if we're in a hurry.

This makes most of us distinctly ill-equipped to be superheroes.

Comic book heroes are defined largely by their willingness to sacrifice themselves for the good of others, in big ways *and* small. Frankly, that's about the only trait these folks share. They can be rich or poor, saints or sinners, leap tall buildings in a single bound or dig under them with a few twists of their neutrino-powered hand shovels. But these heroes—if they're worth the title at all—will take a bullet for the little old lady sitting in the park, even if they don't know said little old lady and the slug is made of kryptonite. Many of them don't just show a willingness to die for their fellow man, they actually *do* die on occasion, only to be brought back to life through some regeneration matrix or sneaky sleight of hand. An example: in 2011, Peter Parker, aka Spider-Man, died in Marvel's *Ultimate Spider-Man* comics but kept right on slinging webs in its *Amazing Spider-Man* series. Superheroes have a hard time resting in peace.

But as sacrificial as all these caped comrades may be, few have given more of themselves than Batman.

## WHAT WILL YOU GIVE ME?

Heroism and sacrifice have been irreversibly soldered together in legends and stories for millennia now, with many of them (intentionally or not) reminding us of Jesus' ultimate sacrifice on the cross. For Christians, or even people raised in a predominantly Christian culture, sacrifice and martyrdom are a huge deal. Beowulf sacrificed himself in his climactic battle with the dragon; Sydney Carton offered himself in Charles Dickens's *A Tale of Two Cities*; Gandalf and Frodo both sacrificed themselves for the greater good in J. R. R. Tolkien's *The Lord of the Rings*. Even when we turn from fiction to historical fact, we're deeply awed by those who have given their lives for a noble cause. More often than not, those are the people we call heroes in our everyday lives. Abraham Lincoln and Martin Luther King Jr., as important as they are and as beloved as they'd be had they not died early, are much more inculcated into our cultural mythos because their lives were claimed by assassins, giving them the allure of martyrs.

But as immeasurably important as it is that Christ died for us, we sometimes forget that he *lived* for us too. He sacrificed his all for us every day he walked the earth, teaching and doing miracles for us when he might have rather been hanging out at his Father's house or even taking a well-deserved break by the sea. His sacrifices took many forms: He was rejected by his own people. He suffered humiliation and scorn for us, endured scarcely imaginable pain, and only when he could give us nothing more of his humanity did he commit his life back into his Father's hand. Through story and song we've learned to get our minds around the idea of sacrificing our lives for someone else and believe we could do it ourselves . . . but I don't think most of us dare conceive of just how far Jesus' sacrifice truly went.

Perhaps in looking at what Batman has given up to serve the citizens of Gotham City, we can begin to get a cursory inkling. While the Dark Knight has put his life and health in jeopardy countless times during his multidecade career, his greatest sacrifices have come in life, not in risking death.

"Dying for something is easy because it is associated with glory," writes Donald Miller in *Blue Like Jazz*. "Living for something . . . is the hard thing. Living for something extends beyond fashion, glory, or recognition. We live for what we believe."

Bruce Wayne, as Batman, lives for what he believes. His new life began, according to his 1939 origin story in *Detective Comics* No. 33 ("The Batman Wars against the Dirigible of Doom") with the trappings of a bedtime prayer. In a later retelling ("Secret Origins Starring the Golden Age Batman," *Secret Origins* No. 6, September 1986), we're given greater detail.

"Don't forget to say your prayers, Bruce," a voice outside Bruce's room intones.

"I *never* forget them, Uncle Philip." And then, with his

hands clasped, tears welling in his eyes, he makes his promise—the promise that will set the cadence for his whole being.

"And I swear by the spirits of my parents to avenge their deaths, by spending the rest of my life *warring on all criminals*!" he says. "*Please*, dear God—help me *keep* my promise! I'll do *anything*!"

Sometimes in our naiveté we try to cut deals with God. We promise that if he gives us such-and-such or takes from us such-and-such, we'll walk in his ways for the rest of our days. We'll never lie. We'll never cheat. We'll do anything if God will give us what we want, what we need, just this one time.

There are elements of this sort of deal-making behavior here. But there's something else at work too. This particular prayer of Bruce's isn't unlike the sort of prayer we offer up to God when we commit our lives to him. We, like Bruce, tell God we can't fulfill our purpose without him. We, like Bruce, beg for help. We, like Bruce, promise God anything and everything—to serve him through our body, mind, and soul. We are essentially turning over the keys to him. We are giving our lives for his purposes, sacrificing our own selfish desires for a greater good.

When you think about that and all its myriad implications, the prospect of becoming a Christian should terrify us a little. Few of us truly understand that when we ask God to drive, he's liable to take us up on our offer.

C. S. Lewis writes in *Mere Christianity*:

The Christian way is different: harder, and easier. Christ says "Give me All. I don't want so much of

your time . . . and so much of your work: I want
You. I have not come to torment your natural self,
but to kill it. No half-measures are any good. I don't
want to cut off a branch here and a branch there,
I want to have the whole tree down. I don't want to
drill the tooth, or crown it, or stop it, but to have it
out. Hand over the whole natural self, all the desires
which you think innocent as well as the ones you
think wicked—the whole outfit. I will give you
a new self instead. In fact, I will give you Myself:
my own will shall become yours."

Bruce Wayne committed himself to something greater
than himself and radically changed the trajectory of his life.
But it would not come without sacrificing, in a sense, Bruce
Wayne. He was given a new will, but in return he gave his all.

## HOW MUCH DO YOU WANT?

The makers of the latest Batman films understand the sacrifices required of someone who follows the sort of strange
path Batman does. And their work is filled with examples of
Bruce Wayne's "generous" nature.

### His Honor

We all know Bruce came from a wealthy, influential family.
And it's not like the Waynes just frittered away their time hunt-
ing foxes and ordering servants around either. According to
the glimpses we get of his family heritage in *Batman Begins*,

Bruce's ancestors were all dynamic do-gooders. Wayne Manor served as a stop on the Underground Railroad during the time of Bruce's great-great-grandfather. Thomas Wayne was a generous philanthropist who spent scads of the family fortune helping Gotham's downtrodden. The Wayne family has been a beacon in the city for a long, long time. Every chance he gets, Alfred tries to impress upon Bruce how important the Wayne moniker is.

When a crisis descends on Wayne Manor during his birthday party in *Batman Begins*, Bruce decides everyone must leave. Immediately. Alfred is aghast.

"Those are Bruce Wayne's guests out there, sir," he says. "You have a name to maintain."

"I don't care about my name," Bruce says.

"It's not just your name, sir," Alfred says, voice quavering. "It's your father's name. And it's all that's left of him. Don't destroy it."

But by necessity, he does. That evening when Ra's al Ghul comes to call, he saves the lives of his guests by insulting them. Affecting an ever-so-slight slur in his voice, he calls them "two-faced friends" and "sycophantic suck-ups," ordering them out of his house before he says something *really* nasty.

"The apple has fallen very far from the tree, Mr. Wayne," a guest says to him on his way out.

Had I been in Bruce Wayne's shoes right then, that throwaway retort would have cut me to the quick. Most of us, I think, spend inordinate energy trying to make our parents proud of us. We want to feel like we're being good stewards of the family name and legacy—whatever that legacy might be.

While no family is perfect, few of us can ever completely shake (nor would we want to) the bonds that tie us to our moms and dads. We love them, and we want to do right by them.

And so, of course, does Bruce. But the only way he can truly follow in his father's philanthropic footsteps—at least in that moment—is by sullying the family rep. And he doesn't stop there. Bruce works overtime to make his public facade seem as selfish and shallow as possible, the antithesis of his near-sainted father. He wants the world to believe that he is, indeed, a bad apple. Yet even as he sacrifices the family name and alienates his father's friends, he would make his father proud, and perhaps his heavenly Father as well.

### His Lamborghini

Laugh if you will. Compared to some things Bruce Wayne has given up, a silver Lamborghini seems fairly low on the list. But it's not the car sacrificed that interests me here but rather Coleman Reese, the man Bruce sacrificed his gas-guzzler for.

Coleman, an accountant tasked with combing through Wayne Enterprises' books, discovers some bizarre discrepancies in the company's applied sciences division. Being good with numbers, he puts two and two together and deduces that Bruce Wayne and Batman are the same person. Eventually, he decides to reveal the secret on a popular Gotham talk show, a move that would surely mean the end of Batman and the imprisonment of Bruce Wayne. But before the accountant can spill the Bat's beans, the Joker cuts in and tells Gotham that Coleman needs to die—curiously defending his archenemy's secret identity. If someone doesn't kill Coleman "in sixty minutes, then I blow up a hospital," says Joker.

The police try to protect Coleman as well as they can, but it's a tall order, given how many Gothamites have friends and relatives in hospital beds. Coleman's death seems a small price to pay to save a loved one's life. As the accountant is transported to a place of safety in a police SUV, a man in a truck revs his engine and guns forward with the idea of killing the civilian inside.

Like a secret service agent taking a bullet, Bruce's fast and furious Lamborghini jets between the pickup and the SUV. The truck crashes into the side of the sports car, totaling it and breaking many a fourteen-year-old boy's heart. But Bruce saves Coleman's life.

"Mr. Wayne, isn't it?" Jim Gordon asks an apparently dazed playboy billionaire after the accident. "That was a very brave thing you did."

"What, trying to catch the light?" Bruce says.

"You weren't protecting the van?" Gordon asks.

"Why, who's in it?"

But then Bruce gives Coleman an ever-so-slight look of recognition. *I know you*, that look seems to say. *I know you could hurt me. Be on your way.*

Bruce Wayne didn't really know Coleman Reese. The only thing he knew about him was that Coleman wanted to do him harm—even destroy him. And Coleman, if he so desired, still could. Bruce didn't put any conditions on his act of sacrifice. He didn't tell Coleman, "Okay, I did you a favor this time . . . but if you cross me again, I'll run you down myself." Most of us, if we learned that a total stranger was trying to hurt or slander us in some way, would take the slimy you-know-who to court—or at least post something demeaning about him on Facebook. Some of us might make a halfhearted effort to save the guy's life . . . if we were in the neighborhood and all. But we'd certainly want some assurance that our sacrifice would benefit us somehow.

Bruce saved Coleman without that assurance, risking his own life, career, identity, and freedom, and totaling a $400,000 car besides. Even if we could afford a fleet of Lamborghinis, few of us would be willing to make that sort of sacrifice for one of our enemies. Yet as Christians, that's what we're called to do.

### His Love

In our last chapter, we watched as the Joker forced Batman to make the horrific choice of either saving Harvey Dent (Gotham's dashing district attorney) or Rachel Dawes (Bruce Wayne's childhood friend and perhaps the love of his life). Joker promised Batman that he'd only have time to reach one of them, and in this case, he wasn't joking.

At first, Batman makes the decision we all assume he will make: he races to save Rachel. But then, en route, he changes his mind and rushes to rescue Harvey. And while the film doesn't definitively answer why Batman wound up rescuing Harvey instead (did the Joker lie to him? did he get confused?), I believe that Batman *chose* to rescue the district attorney. Initially he made the choice any of us would likely make: to save the person closest to us personally. But en route he realized that while Bruce Wayne might need Rachel Dawes, Gotham needed Harvey Dent. And so he changed his plans, making one of the most painful sacrifices of all.

Of all the questionable decisions we see Batman make in *The Dark Knight*, this is the strangest, most inexplicable, perhaps least forgivable. Most of us can grasp the idea of sacrificing ourselves for the sake of those closest to us. But could we sacrifice those closest to us for a hypothetical greater good?

People do make such sacrifices, of course. Soldiers and firefighters and policemen put their lives on the line daily for folks they don't know. It's their job. But would we ask them to man the front lines or stay on duty if their own spouses or families were in jeopardy? It's unthinkable, really. And more than a little cruel.

Other superheroes at other times have faced such a decision. In 2002's *Spider-Man*, the Green Goblin tries to force just such a dilemma on Spidey: save Mary Jane Watson, his love interest, or a trolley full of innocents. Our friendly neighborhood webslinger found a way to save both.

But in *The Dark Knight*, Batman finds no such out. He must choose. And the choice nearly breaks him. Rachel dies, and Harvey, while he makes it out alive, isn't really saved. The loss of Rachel destroys something in his mind and turns him into Two-Face.

"What happened to Rachel wasn't chance," Batman tells Harvey as Jim Gordon looks on. "We decided to act! We three!"

"Then why was it me who was the only one who lost everything?" Dent cries out.

"It wasn't," Batman says.

It's a hard place, this fallen world of ours. And while few of us are asked explicitly to make such a terrible choice, our lives are not often filled with a steady diet of win-win scenarios. People are hurt, people sometimes even die through the manipulation of some and the choices of others. And when we love, we leave ourselves open to the worst sort of loss.

The Bible doesn't sugarcoat this hard reality. Scriptural protagonists suffer soul-rending grief, just as we do—often illustrated through the father's loss (or apparent loss) of a son. Jacob, if you remember, tore his clothes when he thought his beloved son, Joseph, had been killed by wild animals. (Joseph's brothers had actually sold the youth into slavery.) Jacob, refusing to be comforted, cried, "I will go to my grave mourning for my son" (Genesis 37:35). David, the greatest king of Israel, lost his kingdom to his popular but duplicitous son, Absalom. And yet when his rebel son died at the hands of David's soldiers, David was torn in two. "O my son Absalom!" he cried, tears running down his cheeks as he ran to a room overlooking Jerusalem's gateway. "My son, my son Absalom! If only I had died instead of you! O Absalom, my son, my son" (2 Samuel 18:33).

While the Bible acknowledges these kinds of losses, rarely are its players offered up for literal sacrifice. Judaism, unlike many Middle Eastern religions of biblical times, condemned such sacrifice as an abomination. And yet there are times when the theme still surfaces. In one prominent story, Abraham is offered a terrible, impossible choice. And the one asking the hero to make it isn't Joker or Green Goblin but our own Creator. In Genesis 22, God himself tells Israel's patriarch (considered by Jews, Christians, and Muslims to be the founder of their faiths) to "Take your son, your only son—yes, Isaac, whom you love so much—and go to the land of Moriah. Go and sacrifice him as a burnt offering on one of the mountains, which I will show you" (Genesis 22:2). The request sets the stage for one of Scripture's most horrifying and poignant stories—one that came awfully close to a tragic, faith-jarring ending. Abraham nearly does what God requested. But just when the knife's about to fall on Isaac's throat, Abraham hears the angel of the Lord: "Don't lay a hand on the boy! Do not hurt him in any way, for now I know that you truly fear God. You have not withheld from me even your son, your only son" (Genesis 22:12).

The story was not just intended to test Abraham's faith but to tell later readers that this God—unlike other Middle Eastern "deities" who thought nothing of demanding blood from innocent kids—did things a little differently.

But the story serves another purpose: to set the stage for a very different sacrifice. "Your son, your only son," God says to Abraham—a phrase that when I read it, sounds almost like grief . . . grieving not just for Abraham's pain and Isaac's near sacrifice at his hands but perhaps looking ahead and seeing another beloved Son sacrificed in the future: his own.

## Himself

By the time Batman, Dent, and Gordon discuss their losses in *The Dark Knight* in the heart of an old, skeletal warehouse,

Dent has slipped into madness, the darkness has choked the goodness out of him and turned him into Batman's most tragic adversary. Now Two-Face aims to avenge Rachel's death by punishing those he blames for it the only way he knows how—with the flip of a coin.

First the coin judges Batman, landing scarred side up. Two-Face fires a slug into Batman's gut, sending him sprawling. He flips it again, gun pointed this time at his own temple, but the fair side shows up.

Now he prepares to send the coin through the air one last time, judging Commissioner Gordon. Only the gun isn't pointed at the policeman. It's aimed at the head of Gordon's little boy . . . his only son.

"Harvey, you were right," Gordon beseeches. "Rachel's death was my fault. Please don't punish the boy. Please punish me."

"I'm about to," Two-Face tells him. With a flash and a metallic ting, the coin twists into the black night.

But before it can land, Batman gets up from the warehouse floor and slams into Two-Face. The pair fall free of the building. Two-Face apparently dies on impact. Batman survives.

In some superhero narratives, this would be the end of the story, and a relatively happy ending indeed. But endings are rarely tidy in real life, and again, *The Dark Knight* does not embrace the easy out. Dent, Gotham's white knight, isn't just dead; he's corrupted, a crusader turned criminal, guilty of killing innocent people. How can Gordon and Batman begin to make that better?

"The Joker won," Gordon says. "Harvey's prosecution, everything he fought for, undone. . . . The Joker took the best of us and tore him down."

Batman, limping, hurting, refuses to admit defeat. "The Joker cannot win," he says, gently moving Harvey's unmoving face so the streetlights can brush the side unscarred. And then he turns to Gordon and accepts another cross, makes another sacrifice.

"*I* killed those people," he says, taking Harvey's own sin upon his shoulders. "That's what I can be."

"No, you can't!" Gordon says. "You're not!"

"I'm whatever Gotham needs me to be," Batman says. "Call it in."

## INNOCENT GUILT

In ancient Israel, when Jews observed Yom Kippur, the deeply sacred Day of Atonement, priests would select two goats to take part in the ceremonies. One would be offered to God. The other would be kept alive and set loose in the desert as a living sacrifice of atonement, symbolically carrying all the sins of Israel with it into the wilderness.

Before his fall in *The Dark Knight*, Harvey Dent is perhaps who we'd like to be on our best day. He's brave, principled, moral—Batman without all the angst and drama. He's a righteous man who wants to do some good in the world.

But then Dent's thrown off his game by pain and disappointment. He's crushed by the horror of loss, and his heart opens to an evil he cannot comprehend. As a result, he does some nuclear-grade sinning and falls from grace, his face an ugly, awful parody of the beauty that once was. In that moment he represents our fall, individually and collectively, an Adam who has tasted the apple, a Saul throwing spears. He's a glimmer of what all of us must look like to God in the midst of our sins and failings. His sin is stripped of its skin and revealed for the ugliness it is, naked and terrible in the light.

But even after Two-Face's fall, there's still hope. "The Joker cannot win," Batman insists. He touches Dent's face and turns his unblemished side to face the light. And then he tells Gordon that he will take Dent's crimes upon himself, carrying them into Gotham's wilderness with him so that Harvey can be without blemish, without fault, without sin. He becomes, by his own hand, a scapegoat.

I don't think Batman is intended to be a symbol of Jesus here. We know too much about Batman to accept him as a spiritual savior; he has plenty of shortcomings himself. And obviously Batman, unlike Christ, doesn't die for Harvey's sins. He lives for them.

But Batman's sacrifice is an imperfect reflection of part of Jesus' work at the cross. Whatever story lines lie in store for Batman in the future, he'll never be able to perfectly illustrate Christ's role as sacrificial lamb, blameless and unblemished. But he does recall Jesus' role as scapegoat—carrying the weight of our sins on his own back, dragging them as he staggered to Calvary. And in so doing, Batman helps emphasize some of the critical elements of Jesus' sacrifice that we might lose sight of. Most of us who grew up within Christianity know that Christ died for our sins. We know he suffered on the cross. But we sometimes forget all the humiliation and scorn he endured along the way.

Like Batman, Jesus was considered a hero to his people for a time—a man of miracles, a teacher of great authority. Some believed that Jesus might save them all from the horrible world in which they lived, crushing the immoral powers that yoked them and leading Israel to forgotten glory. But then, after one fateful kiss, everything changed. Jesus wasn't a hero anymore but a villain, an enemy of the state. The people abandoned him, and his dearest friends denied him. He was mocked and spat upon, heckled and jeered. Overnight Jerusalem's Savior became its most hated, most despised, perhaps most feared man.

"Jesus is a rejected Messiah," writes Dietrich Bonhoeffer in *The Cost of Discipleship*. "His rejection robs the passion of its halo of glory. It must be a passion without honor. Suffering and rejection sum up the whole cross of Jesus."

And so in this way, maybe Batman and Jesus have a little something in common. Both understood that to do their jobs, they'd have to be willing to sacrifice everything. They'd need to risk scorn and humiliation to do what was right. They'd need to be willing to die. In some ways, perhaps Batman's decision to take to the road was even more difficult. Jesus, after all, knew who he was, knew where he was going, and knew of a grander purpose behind it all. Batman—an imperfect mortal in a fallen world—couldn't have had that level of assurance. He simply knew what he had to do . . . and did it. This doesn't make him a savior, but it does make him a hero. And in the same way, Jesus calls us all to heroism.

Bonhoeffer tells us,

> While it is true that only the sufferings of Christ
> are a means of atonement, yet since he has suffered
> for and borne the sins of the whole world and
> shares with his disciples the fruits of his passion,
> the Christian also has to undergo temptation; we
> too have to bear the sins of others; we too must bear
> their shame and be driven like a scapegoat from the
> gate of the city.

This is the burden that anyone who dares call himself a Christian must carry. Yes, we are saved by grace, but it is a costly grace, in Bonhoeffer's words—one that requires us to submit to God's will and renew our submission every day. And that means being willing to sacrifice—to forsake our own wants and desires for the greater and better. It's not easy. In fact, it can be horribly difficult.

As I've said, I don't do sacrifice very well. Perhaps none of us do. And maybe that's why God asks it of us. Because it's hard. Because we treasure so much that we don't need. Because our pride and possessions and sometimes even our relationships can come between us and him. We love these lives that God has given us . . . perhaps too much at times. And so we forget our business. We forget what we're to be about.

Herein lies the paradox. Just as it truly does feel better to give presents at Christmas than to get them, so run the sacrifices that Jesus asks of us. That doesn't mean there won't be pain or sorrow or anger or grief. But when we leave ourselves open to sacrifice, when we tell God, truthfully, that our lives are his, we find joy.

Jesus tells us in Matthew 10:37-42,

> If you love your father or mother more than you love me, you are not worthy of being mine; or if you love your son or daughter more than me, you are not worthy of being mine. If you refuse to take up your cross and follow me, you are not worthy of being mine. If you cling to your life, you will lose it; but if you give up your life for me, you will find it. Anyone who receives you receives me, and anyone who receives me receives the Father who sent me. . . . And if you give even a cup of cold water to one of the least of my followers, you will surely be rewarded.

Perhaps when we use Batman as an illustration to examine what being a Christian may look like, it's hard to believe Jesus' words. We see the sacrifice but we don't see the reward. We see the pain, but we don't see the joy. Batman has given everything and seems to have gotten nothing in return.

But in spite of our modern age's view of Batman—a hurting, perhaps slightly deranged good guy fighting off his own demons as he fights his ever-present foes—there's something to be said about the life he's chosen. Something beautiful. Something wonderful. And we're about to find out what that is.

## Chapter 10

# HERO

*No; we have been as usual asking the wrong question.*
*It does not matter a hoot what the mockingbird on the*
*chimney is singing. If the mockingbird were chirping*
*to give us the long-sought formulae for a unified field*
*theory, the point would be only slightly less irrelevant.*
*The real and proper question is: Why is it beautiful?*
—Annie Dillard, *Pilgrim at Tinker Creek*

**WE'VE TALKED A LOT** about what makes Batman who he is and why he does what he does. We've seen his scars and felt his sacrifice. We've heard his calling and cracked his code. We've gotten a hint of why he throws batarangs and falls off buildings and glowers at people in the shadows. I think we've heard enough to be dutifully impressed with, if nothing else, his level of commitment—even if we think he could use an occasional visit with a good therapist. In fact, we may know entirely too much about him at this point.

Let's face it: Batman has it tough. Being a costumed crime fighter is a high-risk occupation, where a bad day at the office might involve being hung upside down above a vat of acid, having your memory erased by a super-secret ray gun, or learning that someone just published your true identity on TMZ.

Likewise, being a Christian can be pretty difficult. Granted, it's not nearly as bad now as it was, say, in ancient Rome, or as awkward here as it is in Saudi Arabia. But even in the Western world these days, and in the heart of civilizations founded in Christendom, it's not always cool to be Christian or hip to have faith. Sometimes when you tell people about your beliefs, they look at you funny and maybe even accuse you of being stupid or homophobic or a prig (if you hang out with the sort of folks who use the word *prig* in regular conversation). Others may think you a little . . . different—which just makes sense, really, because if you take your faith seriously, you *will* be different. You should be different. And being different is often pretty hard. Just ask Batman.

At this point, we can almost hear the Joker sidle up beside us and ask us in his creepiest, smarmiest way, "What's the point? Why bother? This faith of yours, it feels like a bad joke. You can't do this, you can't do that, but you *have* to do that *other* thing. All those *rules*. All those *responsibilities*. Haven't you ever just wanted to go a little crazy? Why live like this?"

Well, we already know why Batman resists that kind of talk. He's following his calling, serving a higher purpose. He wants to keep the citizens of Gotham from suffering the sort of loss he did so many years ago.

And yet the question for us doesn't necessarily give way so easily. *Why?* Following a calling doesn't carry the weight it once did, not in a time when the brain is thought to be more machine than mind, at the mercy of its own chemistry and binary code. Not in a time when so many of the people and things and ideals we've believed in have turned out so wrong. Not in a time when our individual happiness is considered, in many respects, the ultimate goal. "A calling?" the Joker would say, inching closer to us. "A higher purpose? You gotta be kidding."

We have the misfortune of living at a time when it's nearly impossible to trust. Cynicism weighs heavy on our souls. We live in an age of scandal, of pedophile priests and wayward pastors, of petty politicians, bombastic pundits, and reality television. Sometimes it's not the stuff in the dark that scares us anymore; it's the stuff that crawls into the light. Who is left to trust? There are those who will say—without pause, without even any real sadness—nobody. Nothing. Charities line their pockets. Ministries play for political power. Maybe Catwoman is right in embracing amorality. After all, no one can be truly charitable, truly giving . . . and anyone who pretends they are is just rationalizing their own misshapen desires and gussying them up with gilded lies. There is no honesty in the world. We can't even be honest with ourselves. We are craven animals pretending to be people, machines that have mistaken their own inner switches for a soul. "Higher calling?" the Joker cackles, twirling a switchblade between his fingers. "Don't make me choke. The only people who would really hear such a calling are crazier than I am."

Which brings us back to Batman, where we open the door on a final paradox.

## GOING BATTY?

When Bruce Wayne throws on a cape and cowl, he can come off as a little extreme. It's not normal to do what he does. It's not quite right. Sane men don't throw on body armor and blast into the dead of night, patrolling the streets for evil-doers. And they certainly don't do it in costume. What did we say at the beginning of this book, that it takes a "special" (read: weird) person to do what Batman does?

We glossed over this weirdness then, but it's time to revisit and examine Batman's state of sanity. We must explore whether everything's completely okay underneath that cowl—whether his heroism is a product of purpose or psychosis, a calling from above or a twisted craving from within. Is Batman a hero, or is Bruce Wayne simply a bat or two short of a belfry?

Certainly, Batman's sanity has been on the table for a while now. Authors have toyed with Bruce's state of mind in *Arkham Asylum: A Serious House on Serious Earth*, the noncanonical *Batman: The Dark Knight Returns*, and scads of other narratives. In the film *Batman Returns*, Selina Kyle tells Bruce Wayne that she likes him because he's different. "Sickos never scare me," she says. "At least they're commit-ted." In *The Dark Knight*, the Joker invites Batman to room with him at Arkham Asylum.

Even Bruce Wayne himself isn't above contemplating his own mental wherewithal. "A guy who dresses up like a bat clearly has issues," he says during dinner in *Batman Begins*. And so the psychoanalysis begins. Is his commitment a form of mania? Is his dour demeanor a sign of depression? Is he out of control? *Too* controlled?

But Alfred in 1993's animated *Batman: Mask of the Phantasm* is having none of it. "Why, you're the very model of sanity," he reassures Bruce. "Oh, by the way, I pressed your tights and put away your exploding gas balls."

All this talk about whether Batman's crazy—whether he's a hero or just off his rocker—reminds me a little of what C. S. Lewis famously said about Jesus in *Mere Christianity*:

> A man who was merely a man and said the sort of things Jesus said would not be a great moral teacher. He would either be a lunatic—on the level with the man who says he is a poached egg—or else he would be the Devil of Hell. You must make your choice. Either this man was, and is, the Son of God: or else a madman or something worse. You can shut Him up for a fool, you can spit at Him and kill Him as a demon; or you can fall at His feet and call Him Lord and God. But let us not come with any patronizing nonsense about His being a great human teacher. He has not left that open to us. He did not intend to.

It makes me wonder: is there just something about living a life of purpose that looks a little loony to our jaded, twenty-first century eyes?

There are, of course, those who think that faith itself is a frightening mental imbalance. Famous nonbelievers—from

Madalyn Murray O'Hair (founder of American Atheists) to Bill Maher (comedian and cocreator of the film *Religulous*)—have said so, imploring us to drop our dangerous devotion and instead to pick up a cross of rationalism. Biologist Richard Dawkins pinned the theme of an entire book (*The God Delusion*) on the premise. Religion is frightening because it's illogical and irrational, they say. It makes people do strange, incomprehensible things—things that normal, sane people just don't do.

They're right, of course. Faith *is* a little crazy—like love or hope or passion.

Please don't misunderstand: there are loads of reasons to believe in God, countless reasons to be a Christian. For two thousand years, eminently rational men—some of the brightest folks of their or any century—have accepted and outlined those reasons. The core of our faith is logical and reasonable. But in the end, we must admit that it is also unreasonable. Or, more precisely, that it transcends reason, just as all beautiful things do.

Secularists will counter that religion has been the catalyst for some of the planet's bloodiest conflicts and most vicious atrocities. And that is true. Christianity itself has a long, sordid past loaded with shameful, even damning acts. Ra's al Ghul, as we've seen, can be used as an example of religious fervor gone awry. And let's not kid ourselves that we're immune to righteous overreach ourselves. If we take our faith seriously and embrace it passionately, there's some danger we could take it all too far.

We see it every now and then in Batman himself. Faith

is powerful, like fire, wave, or storm. Faith is life, breath, and magic. But faith can also be perilous. We are filled with the spark of the one who made us, and while his spark can be a great resource for good, it can also cause greater destruction when it is misused. The Spirit within us is wild and restless, and when our own fallible natures misunderstand, misuse, and corrupt the spark God has given us, horrible sins and godless ideals (that we sometimes mistakenly attribute to God) can be the ugly results. Our heaven-born spark, mixed with hellish intent, can be combustible indeed.

But believers can no more snuff out the Spirit in us than we could stop eating (for fear of poison) or drinking (for fear of drowning). We may live in a world in which we lose sight of our Creator, but he never loses sight of us, and we can never extricate ourselves from his design and purpose. We are his whether we acknowledge it or not. We are made to be vessels of light—hurricane lamps for a greater will. And in the end it's awfully hard for us to really deny that purpose, to squelch that flickering flame of faith.

Not that we don't try sometimes. And some have gotten so good at dirtying or hiding or simply shutting their eyes to the light that when they see it in others, they don't understand it—like some people don't understand love or music. They can't comprehend it. It doesn't make sense. It's not reasonable, not rational. And so they call it crazy, call it dangerous, call it terrible names in hopes of dispelling it, like an evil spirit to be cast from their presence.

But the light remains. The truth is too strong.

## DISPELLING THE DARKNESS

Only in an insane world—or, perhaps, in a world too sane for its own good—would we call a hero crazy for being a hero. We can take issue with Batman's methods and can certainly quibble with his costume, but the hero remains, and most of us, Christian or not, see him for who he is. We can't deny his goodness.

"Goodness!" the Joker might exclaim. "There is no such thing!" "You see, their morals, their code, it's a bad joke," he tells Batman in *The Dark Knight*. "They're only as good as the world allows them to be. I'll show you. When the chips are down, these . . . these civilized people, they'll eat each other."

As is often the case, the Joker has a point. When the chips are down, goodness just doesn't make sense for us. If we look at things with a purely rational, scientific, naturalistic eye, our vices make more sense than our virtues, our bad habits seem more rational than our best inclinations. Sex, from a purely procreational, preserve-the-species point of view, is incredibly logical. Love is not. Our impulse for gluttony, given a history accursed with a chronic scarcity of food, makes tons of sense. Charity—the giving of our food or wealth or belongings to complete strangers—does not. Taking the life of someone who threatens us, given our instinct for self-preservation and the constant competition for resources, would seem sensical. The saving of that same life? Daft.

Greed, envy, sloth—the roots of all these deadly sins are easily traced to our animal selves or biological programming. They are what come naturally to us. And while scientists are trying to uncover the evolutionary reasoning behind kindness, altruism, grace, and goodness, it's a far more difficult task. Our celebration of these things seems almost akin to celebrating our appendixes and belly buttons as the most intrinsic, most beautiful, and most hallowed of all our body organs.

To hold the values that we do seems almost . . . crazy.

Unless we are not merely naturalistic mechanisms—animals living to eat and breed, organisms that merely long to sate our hungers and salve our pains. Unless we all hear a calling beyond our understanding or understand a code given to us from another, barely fathomable source.

Heroism is unnatural unless there is another nature. Unless there is another reality that we ultimately call our home.

## THE JOY OF SACRIFICE

"Excuse me—you're ignoring my question," the Joker tells us. "Why? Even with this 'other reality,' why would you ever follow its call? Batman, he's miserable! Trust me, I know. You've as much as admitted it yourself. He's sacrificed everything for this 'call' of his. He struggles with pain and doubt. He adheres to a code that would seem horribly dull. Why? Why? Why!"

In the *No Man's Land* saga, Batman returns to a nearly empty and wholly chaotic Gotham City. After having left the city for months, Batman comes back to bring some sanity into this insane nightscape.

"The work, sir," Alfred tells him, walking along a

car-choked bridge with the Dark Knight. "It's about the work. There's much to do. And if not us, sir, then who?"

"Yes, who?" Batman says darkly, echoing everything we know about his purpose and code, his struggle and sacrifice.

But then Alfred hints at another motivation.

"It's been too long since we've seen you in action, sir," he says. "You looked good. Did it feel good?"

"No, Alfred," Batman says. "It felt *great*."

Modern renditions of Batman have painted a gloomy portrait of the Dark Knight, a silent, solemn superhero who'd rather go three rounds with Bane than crack a smile. And while this shadowy, solitary figure fits modern sensibilities, it has almost obliterated the sense that there could be a little bit of fun in this crazy gig of his too. That maybe, just maybe, Batman likes the work.

For decades, his joy was obvious. In the comics in the 1940s, '50s, and '60s, Batman was a smiling superhero— believe it or not—always ready with a wisecrack or spectacularly bad pun. This was no tortured antihero, no brooding bat. He was still engaged in serious work, but his sense of fun was palpable. When *Batman* showed up on television in 1966, our Dark Knight had become a comic crusader. And even as he grew more serious in the comics of the 1970s, there were still outlets in which Batman looked like he was having the time of his life. *Super Friends* was one. There was the Batman I first knew and loved and pretended to be. No seven-year-old wants to spend recess glowering. And we still see hints of that joy in Batman, even when he's swathed in shadow.

In *Batman Begins*, Alfred tells Bruce Wayne that if he

*pretended* to have fun, he might have a little by accident. And maybe he does. But the real joy he feels doesn't come in the guise of Bruce the billionaire playboy. It comes as Batman—when he does what he was meant to do. When he follows his purpose.

There is a joy that comes from purpose, a pleasure indescribable when we stop fighting to have our own way and settle down to serve. "I was not born to be free," C. S. Lewis writes in one of his letters. "I was born to adore and obey." And yet within that obedience comes freedom. It's a paradox Batman knows well, I think.

"Dear brothers and sisters, I plead with you to give your bodies to God because of all he has done for you. Let them be a living and holy sacrifice—the kind he will find acceptable. This is truly the way to worship him," Paul writes in his letter to the Romans (Christians who lived in a place not wholly unlike Gotham City). "Don't copy the behavior and customs of this world, but let God transform you into a new person by changing the way you think" (Romans 12:1-2).

Bruce Wayne sacrificed himself to a cause both high and worthy. He set aside his own ambitions and desires to do a greater work. In a way, he died to himself—pushed away Bruce Wayne and was reborn under a cape and cowl. And then, as Batman, he began to serve a city that perhaps didn't deserve him.

And until the city no longer needs his services, Batman wouldn't have it any other way.

"Why?" the Joker asks.

The answer, in the end, is so simple.

Batman sacrifices and serves because that's what he was

*meant* to do—what God, I'll assert, designed him to do. It's what the guy is gifted at and what he has trained himself to be. Like a Lamborghini is built to race and a plane is built to fly, Bruce Wayne is built to be Batman. And because it's what he is built to do, he loves to do it.

If the Joker came by and asked me why I'm a Christian, I think the answer would be much the same. It's not about proof or apologetics or my upbringing or heaven or hell or anything else.

Why am I Christian? Because I believe I was built to adore and obey. Because when I stray from that state of adoration, I feel the conflict in my soul. Because when I finally, sometimes painfully, submit to God, I feel the joy of his love and grace in the pit of my gut. Because when I curl up in the cup of God's hand, I want to smile. Because when I sense his presence in the world around me, I want to sing. Because when I do what I was meant to do, I feel not just *my* joy but *his* flowing through my arteries like quicksilver.

I am a Christian because even though I'm not a very good Christian at times, I can't imagine life any other way.

The psalmist says,

Shout with joy to the LORD, all the earth!
　Worship the LORD with gladness.
　Come before him, singing with joy.
Acknowledge that the LORD is God!
　He made us, and we are his.
　We are his people, the sheep of his pasture.

PSALM 100:1-3

We are all, I think, called to a life a little like Batman's—a life of struggle and sacrifice, of hardships and heroism. And, thankfully, joy—a joy we find only when we do what we're made to do and worship the one who made us that way. There will be differences, naturally. Luckily, few of us will need to fight bazooka-toting bad guys or brave the wattage of nefarious death rays. On the downside, we won't ever get to cruise around in the Batmobile, either. Superficially, our own callings will look quite a bit different.

But are we asked to sacrifice? To serve others? Are we asked to give our very lives for what we believe in and what we know, in the core of our beings, we're meant to do? I think we are.

This world of ours is a needy place, filled with hurting people who could use what you have to offer. It's not a fair world. It's not a just world.

But it is a world that could use a few more heroes.

# ACKNOWLEDGMENTS

Writing books isn't much like being a superhero. If a schoolkid opted to tail me for a "career day" project, he'd likely collapse of boredom by 2 p.m. But there are, perhaps, some small similarities between the average author and our man in black: we tend to be solitary souls, prone to brooding in cave-like studies and glowering at our computer screens for hours at a time. But while we writers may think of ourselves as loners, we never really do anything alone. This book came about thanks to the efforts and affections of many people.

I owe a great deal of thanks to Steve Isaac, who read and edited every single word of this book and helped protect me from both heresy and bad punctuation; Jonathan Schindler, my editor at Tyndale and fellow "Bat-fan," who made sure my theology was on point, my narratives were coherent, and that I didn't overuse the word *folks*; Joel Kneedler, my agent at Alive Communications, who encouraged me to try my hand at book writing, helped walk me through the bewildering publishing world, and encouraged me every step of the way; Steve Rabey, my mentor and friend, who helped hone my concept and shepherded me through the book's dubious first steps; and Jon Farrar and all the folks at Tyndale House Publishers, who took a chance on working with an unknown, first-time writer in the midst of a pretty dicey economic environment. Thanks, too, to my family, friends, and colleagues, who patiently put up with me during this time.

Finally, thanks to Wendy, my long-suffering wife. Without you, I'm pretty sure I'd be wandering the streets of Reno, selling off my organs one by one. I don't deserve someone as kind and patient and supportive and fun to be with as you . . . but I'll take it.